# BASIC CONNECTIONS

# BASIC CONNECTIONS

## MAKING YOUR JAPANESE FLOW

### Kakuko Shoji

KODANSHA INTERNATIONAL
Tokyo • New York • London

Distributed in the United States by Kodansha America, Inc.,
575 Lexington Avenue, New York, N.Y. 10022, and in the
United Kingdom and continental Europe by Kodansha Europe
Ltd., 95 Aldwych, London WC2B 4JF. Published by Kodansha
International Ltd., 17-14 Otowa 1-chome, Bunkyo-ku, Tokyo
112-8652, and Kodansha America, Inc.

First edition, 1997
00 01 02 03 04 05   10 9 8 7 6 5 4 3
ISBN 4-7700-1968-8

# CONTENTS

# Preface

The purpose of this book is to provide helpful information about Japanese expressions and usages that facilitate the flow of ideas and thought in written and spoken Japanese.

During my thirty-year teaching career, I have seen a great variety of mistakes, many of which were the result of cultural differences or differences in the way that second-language learners and native speakers of Japanese conceptualize language. The book attempts to help students become aware of these differences in conceptualization and to provide them with the linguistic tools to overcome these differences, thereby allowing their ideas to flow more naturally. The book focuses on those grammatical items, idiomatic expressions, and set phrases that have proven to be the most problematic to my students.

The patterns are presented with examples, and tips are provided throughout the text to highlight particularly important points. A few exercises are also included to allow students an opportunity to experiment with what they have learned.

Note that Ⓕ refers to patterns that are predominantly feminine and Ⓜ to those predominantly masculine.

*

I would like to thank the Center of Japanese Studies at the University of Hawai'i for the Japanese Studies Summer Grant (1994) which supported this project. I would also like to thank Greg Nishihara and Sarina Chugani for their hours of computer work and to express appreciation to family and friends for their encouragement and moral support. Very special thanks go to my teachers, Dr. Shiro Hattori and Prof. Fumiko Koide, and to my father, who gave me the opportunity to study and teach abroad and without whom none of this would have been possible. Finally, I would like to express my sincere gratitude to Mr. Michael Brase and Mr. Shigeyoshi Suzuki of Kodansha International, Ltd.; without their help, this publication would not have been possible.

# はじめに

この本は日本語を第二外国語として学ぶ方々、特に初級・中級の学習者を主な読者として書きました。本書のねらいは、日本語の発想や思考の自然な流れを学んでいただき、ネイティヴの日本語感覚に少しでも近づいていただくところにあります。日本語でも英語でもある程度学習した経験のある人なら、この二つの言葉の間には考え方の相違や言葉のシステムの違いからくるズレや問題がいたるところに存在するのをご存じだと思います。三十年以上ハワイ大学で日本語の読み書きを教えてきて、その間違いやつまずきがどこでどんなふうに起こるのか、およその法則性あるいは傾向があることに気がつきました。

　この本では学習者のつまずきを文法的なものと単語や表現に関連するものとに大別して扱っています。文法事項では、やはり「て・に・を・は」を理解するのはなかなか難しいようで、修飾と被修飾の関係、文章と文章が助詞を介してどのようにつながっていくかなどを豊富な例文で説明しました。単語や表現の関連では考え方が異なるため間違いやすい単語や覚えにくいフレーズを用例を示しながら解説しています。本書で用いた例文は実際に学習者が間違えたり、覚えるのに手間取ったりしたものばかりで、これまでに私が集めたものです。なお、独習者が自分で理解度をチェックできるようExercises を用意しました。

　日本語を教えるという環境も今と昔ではおよそ隔世の感が

あります。私がハワイ大学で教鞭をとりはじめた1959年、ハワイが米国の５０番目の州となり、ハワイ大学は州立大学となりました。当時日本語を選択する学生は、進駐軍として日本に行ったことのある元 GI の人たちが大半で、私は先生というより「敗戦国の女」という目で見られることの方が多かったように思います。まだ教師としての経験が浅かった私には、日本語を教えることはほんとうに大変な仕事でした。あれから三十余年、いまでは自分の子供くらいの学生たちが一生懸命日本語を勉強しています。この本が日本語を学んでいる学生たちの助けになり、日本語を教えていく方々にも何らかの参考になれば幸いです。

　この本を書くにあたっては、多くの人々にご協力をいただきました。研究費を支給してくださったハワイ大学の日本研究センター、助手をしてくれた学生のグレッグ西原さんとサリナチュガニさん。また、そもそもこうしてハワイで日本語教師をしていられるのは、恩師服部四郎先生、小出詞子先生そして留学を許してくれた父のおかげです。家族にも大変世話になりました。改めて皆様に感謝の意を表したいと思います。最後にこの本の出版を可能にしてくださった講談社インターナショナルのマイケル・ブレイズさん、鈴木重好さんに厚く御礼申し上げます。

1997 年 2 月

庄司香久子

# BASIC SENTENCE PATTERNS

There are two basic types of sentences in Japanese, the "A is B" type and the "A does B" type. In the "A is B" type, noun or adjectival phrases are linked by a form of the copula だ／です [*da/desu*]. In the "A does B" type, a verb is present, together with nouns or noun phrases.

## ■ "A Is B" Type

An "A is B" sentence does not have a verb and is therefore called a verbless sentence. When B is a noun or noun phrase, B tells what or who A is. For example:

> カマロはアメリカの車だ。
>  A      B
>
> *Kamaro wa Amerika no kuruma da.*
> The Camaro is an American car.

> ピーターはフランスからの留学生です。
>  A      B
>
> *Pītā wa Furansu kara no ryūgakusei desu.*
> Peter is an exchange student from France.

When B is adjectival, B describes A:

> 秋子さんの家はとても大きいです。
>  A         B
>
> *Akiko-san no ie wa totemo ōkii desu.*
> Akiko's house is very big.

<u>この</u>いちごは<u>甘くておいしい</u>です。
  A          B

<u>*Kono ichigo*</u> wa <u>*amakute oishii*</u> desu.
These strawberries are sweet and tasty.

In an "A is B" sentence, the topic marker は [*wa*] and/or the copula だ／です [*da/desu*] may be deleted if their presence is understood from the context:

ユカ:    わたしはおすしをもらうけど、あなたは何にするの？

マリー:  わたし、てんぷら。魚、嫌いなの。

*Yuka:*    *Watashi wa osushi o morau kedo, anata wa nani ni suru no?*

*Marī:*    *Watashi, tenpura. Sakana, kirai na no.*

Yuka:    I'll take the sushi. What are you going to have?

Marie:   I'll have the tempura. I don't like fish (that's why).

In the example above, Marie dropped the particle and copula because their presence is understood from the flow of the conversation. The full form of Marie's statement would be わたしはてんぷらです。（わたしは）魚が嫌いなのです。[*Watashi wa tenpura desu. (Watashi wa) Sakana ga kirai na no desu.*]

---

• Two Uses of です [*desu*]

In the last example, the です [*desu*] of （わたしは）魚が嫌いなのです [*(Watashi wa) Sakana ga kirai na no desu*] merely makes the sentence formal instead of colloquial, while the です [*desu*] of わたしはてんぷらです [*Watashi wa tenpura desu*] is substituting for a verb phrase such as （てんぷら）をもらいます [*Tenpura o moraimasu.* I'll take ~], （てんぷら）にします [*Tenpura ni shimasu.* I've decided on ~], or （てんぷら）がいいです [*Tenpura ga ii desu.* I prefer/want to eat ~].

When a comma immediately follows a noun—as in わたし、てんぷら [*Watashi, tenpura*] and 魚、嫌いなの *Sakana, kirai na no*] in the example above—it often indicates that a particle has been deleted. While punctuation in Japanese is generally not as fixed as in English, this is one instance that is useful to keep in mind.

---

- Omitted Particles & Copulas

When the copula substitutes for a verb, the preceding particle is often deleted.

Q: 何で行くんですか。
A: わたしはバス<u>です</u>（で行きます）。
*Q: Nani de iku n' desu ka.*
*A: Watashi wa basu <u>desu</u> (de ikimasu).*
Q: How are you going?
A: (I'm going) by bus.

Q: 日本ではどこにいらっしゃるんですか。
A: 東京と大阪<u>です</u>（に行きます）。
*Q: Nihon de wa doko ni irassharu n' desu ka.*
*A: Tōkyō to Ōsaka <u>desu</u> (ni ikimasu).*
Q: Where are you going in Japan?
A: (I'll go to) Tokyo and Osaka.

---

In more informal or casual situations, the copula may also be deleted:

わたしはバスです。     *Watashi wa basu desu.*
  ⇨ わたしはバス。     ⇨ *Watashi wa basu.*
  ⇨ わたし、バス。     ⇨ *Watashi, basu.*
  ⇨ バス。     ⇨ *Basu.*

東京と大阪からです。     *Tōkyō to Ōsaka kara desu.*
  ⇨ 東京と大阪から。     ⇨ *Tōkyō to Ōsaka kara.*

Natural Japanese avoids mentioning or repeating what is understood from context.

## ■ "A Does B" Type

A typical "A does B" type sentence consists of a verb phrase and one or more noun phrases. The following is the typical structure of an "A does B" sentence:

| Topic | Subject | Indirect Object | Direct Object | Adverbials | Verb | Sentence Particles |
|-------|---------|-----------------|---------------|------------|------|--------------------|
| は | が | に | を | | | よ, ね, etc. |
| *wa* | *ga* | *ni* | *o* | | | *yo, ne* |

Some examples:

友達が／（わたしに）／彼の／電話番号を／内証で／教えてくれた／の。

*Tomodachi ga / (watashi ni) / kare no / denwa-bangō o / naisho de / oshiete kureta / no.*

My friend secretly told me his telephone number.

母が／弟に／バスケットボールを／買ってやったんだ／よ。Ⓜ

*Haha ga / otōto ni / basuketto-bōru o / katte yatta n' da / yo.*

14

My mother bought a basketball for my younger brother.

When the subject or object is the same as the topic, it is deleted:

わたしは~~わたしが~~本を買います。
*Watashi wa ~~watashi ga~~ hon o kaimasu.*
As for me, I'll buy a book.

本はわたしが~~本を~~買います。
*Hon wa watashi ga ~~hon o~~ kaimasu.*
As for the book, I'll buy it.

In the next two examples, the topic and subject are different, so both appear:

わたしは本が買いたい。
*Watashi wa hon ga kaitai.*
As for me, I want to buy a book.

ここのレストランはてんぷらがおいしい。
*Koko no resutoran wa tenpura ga oishii.*
As for this restaurant, the tempura is good.

Normally, the topic comes at the beginning of the sentence and the main verb comes at the end. The word order, however, is not always fixed, and particles help to indicate the grammatical function when a word appears in an unexpected position. Some examples:

会ったことがあるのか、あの男に？ Ⓜ
*Atta koto ga aru no ka, ano otoko ni?*
Have you met that man before?

わたし、前に見たことがあるんです、あの男（を）。
*Watashi, mae ni mita koto ga aru n' desu, ano otoko (o).*

I have seen that man before.

あんなに高いからって言ったのに、買っちゃったの、
あなた（は）？

*Anna ni takai kara tte itta no ni, katchatta no, anata (wa)?*

Even though I told you it was expensive (so you shouldn't
buy it), you bought it anyway, did you!?

The above examples show that the word order in Japanese can sometimes change rather freely. As explained below,
though, there are cases when the order cannot be changed.

## ■ Modifiers and Modified

In English, a modifying sentence (i.e., relative clause) comes
after the modified noun, while in Japanese the modifying
sentence always comes before the modified word, regardless
of how long the modifier is.

<u>きのう来た</u>手紙

<u>*kinō kita*</u> *tegami*

the letter <u>that came yesterday</u>

<u>ジョンの借りている</u>アパート

<u>*Jon no karite iru*</u> *apāto*

the apartment <u>that John is renting</u>

---

*Exercise 1*

Translate the following sentence literally, and identify
the noun modifiers.

やっと寺の許しを得た三人が布を解いて取り出した仏
像は、今までの仏像とも異った、神秘的な笑みをうか
べた観音像だった。

---

*Yatto tera no yurushi o eta sannin ga nuno o toite tori-
dashita butsuzō wa, ima made no butsuzō to mo koto-
natta, shinpi-teki na emi o ukabeta kannon-zō datta.*

Hint: This is an "A is B" sentence, where A is 仏像
[*butsuzō*] and B is 観音像 [*kannon-zō*]. The gist of the
meaning is, "The three people were finally given permission from the temple, so they undid the cloth and
took out the Buddhist statue. It was a Kannon statue
with a mysterious smile unlike any they had seen before."

For those at an advanced level who need to read Japanese
texts, analyzing sentence structures correctly is essential. Ignoring sentence analysis may make it hard to grasp the content.

In reading, it is important to look for the verb-noun (V-N)
sequences. They will help you pinpoint the modifiers and
modified. Here are some clues to help you.

## ✎ Step 1: Look for V-N Sequences

The first step in identifying the modifiers and modified in a
sentence is to look for verbs that come directly before nouns.
Here are two examples:

ここはいつか友人たちとキャンプに<u>来た</u> <u>所</u>だ。
                             V  N

*Koko wa itsuka yūjin-tachi to kyanpu ni <u>kita</u> <u>tokoro</u> da.*
This is the place where I came with several friends.

わたしは昨年友人がインドネシアから<u>買って来てくれた</u>
                                                 V

<u>絵</u>が好きです。
N

*Watashi wa sakunen yūjin ga Indoneshia kara <u>katte kite</u>*
<u>*kureta*</u> *e ga suki desu.*

I like the picture that my friend (bought and) brought
back for me from Indonesia last year.

## ∞ Step 2: Look for the Subjects, Objects, Modifiers, or Adverbials

The next step is to identify the subjects, objects, modifiers,
and adverbials in the sentence. Remember that the topic
(marked by は [*wa*]) is always outside the modifying clause.
For example:

これは／友達が／去年／インドネシアで／<u>買ってきてくれた</u> シャツです。

| | Subj. | Adv. | Adv. | | V | N | |
|---|---|---|---|---|---|---|---|
| A | | (Modifiers) | | | B | | is. |

*Kore wa / tomodachi ga / kyonen / Indoneshia de / <u>katte</u>*
<u>*kite kureta*</u> *shatsu desu.*

This is the shirt that my friend (bought and) brought back
for me from Indonesia last year.

## ∞ Step 3: Look for Adjectives and Adjectival Nouns

Finally, identify adjectives and adjectival nouns that precede
nouns. Check if the adjectival element has a subject marked
by the subject marker が [*ga*] or の [*no*]. Examples:

<u>髪の毛が長い</u> <u>女の子</u>
<u>*kami no ke ga nagai*</u> <u>*onna no ko*</u>
a girl with long hair (lit., a girl whose hair is long)

<u>人の多い</u> <u>所</u>
<u>*hito no ōi*</u> <u>*tokoro*</u>
a crowded place (lit., a place where there are many people)

実行が不可能な事
*jikkō ga fukanō na koto*
a matter that is impossible to implement (lit., a matter for
　which implementation is impossible)

わたしの好きな花
*watashi no suki na hana*
my favorite flower (lit., the flower that I like)

---

- Adjectives as Verbs

Adjectives and adjectival nouns precede the modified
noun and function like modifying verbs:

おいしいパイ
*oishii pai*
a pie that is delicious / delicious pie

おすしの高くない店
*osushi no takaku nai mise*
a restaurant where sushi is not expensive

おもしろかった映画
*omoshirokatta eiga*
a movie that was interesting

---

# ■ Uses of の [no] and ん [n]

The particle の [*no*] and its variant ん [*n*] have several dis-
tinct uses.

## ◆◆ Connecting Noun Phrases

1. When の [*no*] links a specific noun to a common noun, it
may be translated as "of," "for," "in," or a possessive:

| 私の本 | 花子さんの犬 |
|---|---|
| *watashi no hon* | *Hanako-san no inu* |
| my book / a book of mine | Hanako's dog |

| 東京の大学 | 日本の歴史 |
|---|---|
| *Tōkyō no daigaku* | *Nihon no rekishi* |
| a university in Tokyo | the history of Japan |

2. When の [*no*] links two common nouns, it may be translated as "for," "concerning," "of," "in," etc.

| 男の子の下駄 | きのうのこと |
|---|---|
| *otoko no ko no geta* | *kinō no koto* |
| *geta* for boys | the event of yesterday |

社会の秩序
*shakai no chitsujo*
social order

3. When a common noun precedes の [*no*] and a specific noun, it may be translated as an appositive or a noun modifier:

学生の息子
*gakusei no musuko*
my son, a student / my son the student

友達のジョージ
*tomodachi no Jōji*
George, my friend / my friend George

国立大学の東京大学
*kokuritsu-daigaku no Tōkyō-daigaku*
the University of Tokyo, a national university / the state-run college the University of Tokyo

オペラのカルメン

*opera no Karumen*
*Carmen*, the opera / the opera *Carmen*

4. When の [*no*] follows a noun and a particle, it is generally not translated. Note that a phrase with a particle or with a -て [*-te*] form is considered to be a noun phrase.

東京からの手紙
*Tōkyō kara no tegami*
a letter from Tokyo

イギリスからのペギー
*Igirisu kara no Pegī*
Peggy from England

父へのプレゼント
*chichi e no purezento*
a present for my father

オレゴンまでの切符
*Oregon made no kippu*
a ticket to Oregon

## ❧ Subject Marker

The subject marker が [*ga*] can be replaced by の [*no*] in modifying phrases.

桜ん坊の実のなる頃になりました。
*Sakuranbo no mi no naru koro ni narimashita.*
It has become the time of year when cherries appear.

父のくれたオルゴール
*chichi no kureta orugōru*
the music box that my father gave me

私の好きな人
*watashi no suki na hito*
the person I like

## ❧ Nominalizer

When の [*no*] comes after the dictionary form of a verb, it turns that verb into a noun.

帰るのがすっかり遅くなってしまった。

*Kaeru no ga sukkari osoku natte shimatta.*

Our return home has gotten very late.

彼がワイキキを歩いているのを見た。

*Kare ga Waikiki o aruite iru no o mita.*

I saw him walking along Waikiki.

行くのか行かないのかはっきりしなさい。

*Iku no ka ikanai no ka hakkiri shinasai*

Stop being wishy-washy about whether you are going or
not.

## ✏ Pronominal

Identifying the pronominal の [*no*] is especially important in
reading a longer "A is B"–type sentence. In the following examples, the の [*no*] in the first sentence can be identified
from the context or the situation. In sentences like the second
and third examples, it should be noted that the sentences are
A は [*wa*] B です/だ/である [*desu/da/de aru*] type sentences
which equates to the English "A is B" sentence. When A has
the pronominal の [*no*], B defines or describes A. In the second example, B is a place name, so it defines the の [*no*] in A
as substituting for 所 [*tokoro*; place]. In the third example,
Charles Darwin is a person, so A performs the function of replacing 人 [*hito*; person].

去年 行ったの (は), 有馬だったっけ？

*Sakunen itta no (wa), Arima datta kke?*

Did we go to Arima last year ? (lit., Was the place where
we went last year Arima?)

あそこにあるのは 高そうです。

*Asoko ni aru no wa takasō desu.*

That one over there looks expensive. (lit., The one that is placed over there looks expensive.)

サンゴ礁の進化の段階を最初に明らかにしたのはあの
チャールス・ダーウィンである。

*Sango-shō no shinka no dankai o saisho ni akiraka ni shita
no wa ano Chārusu Dāuin de aru.*

The first one to clarify the evolutionary stages of coral
reefs was Charles Darwin.

#### ➔ Explanatory

Before the copula だ／です／である [*da/desu/de aru*], the
particle の [*no*] shows that the speaker is asking for or giving
an explanation or trying to convince the other person. In
speech, this の [*no*] often becomes ん [*n*].

どうしてそんなことを言ったの（ですか）？
*Dōshite sonna koto o itta no (desu ka)?*
Why did you say something like that?

和子は数学が苦手なのだ。
*Kazuko wa sūgaku ga nigate na no da.*
(Because) Kazuko's no good at mathematics.

せっかく来たんだから、もうしばらくいたら？
*Sekkaku kita n' da kara, mō shibaraku itara?*
Since you've gone to all the trouble to come, why don't
you stay a little longer?

#### ➔ Softener

In formal speech, の [*no*] is added to the ends of sentences to
make questions and statements softer or less direct. の [*no*]
after a statement is normally used by women.

なぜ行かないの？

*Naze ikanai no?*
Why aren't you going?

そう、みんな行くの。
*Sō, minna iku no.*
Yes, everybody's going.

これ、いくらするの？
*Kore, ikura suru no?*
How much is this?

# ■ は [wa] and が [ga]

The particles は [*wa*] and が [*ga*] are perhaps the most troublesome and confusing particles for students to learn. Some students think that both は [*wa*] and が [*ga*] are subject markers and are interchangeable. In fact, though, は [*wa*] marks the sentence's topic or focus, which may be different from the subject of the verb. However, when the topic is the same as the verb's subject or object, は [*wa*] may replace the subject marker が [*ga*] or the object marker を [*o*].

Compare the examples below.

(a) わたしがその本を買った。
*Watashi ga sono hon o katta.*
I (am the one who) bought the book.

わたしはその本を買った。
*Watashi wa sono hon o katta.*
(As for me,) I bought the book.

わたしはその本は買った。
*Watashi wa sono hon wa katta.*
(As for me,) I bought that book (not another book).

その本はわたしが買った。

*Sono hon <u>wa</u> watashi <u>ga</u> katta.*
(As for that book,) I bought it.

(b) わたし<u>は</u>買った時に30ドル払いました。
*Watashi <u>wa</u> katta toki ni sanjū-doru haraimashita.*
(As for me,) I paid $30 when I bought it.

本<u>は</u>買った時に30ドル払いました。
*Hon <u>wa</u> katta toki ni sanjū-doru haraimashita.*
(As for the book,) I paid $30 when I bought it.

When both the subject and the topic are in the sentence, the topic normally precedes the subject. A sentence such as わたしがその本は買いました [*Watashi ga sono hon wa kaimashita*] sounds awkward.

As a topic marker, は [*wa*] may also be used with other particles:

カレンさんからの電話<u>には</u>出たくありません。
*Karen-san kara no denwa <u>ni wa</u> detaku arimasen.*
I don't want to answer phone calls from Karen. (I don't mind answering the phone if it is from someone else.)

One of the functions of は [*wa*] and が [*ga*] is similar to that of the English articles "a" and "the." Like the indefinite article "a," が [*ga*] introduces a new subject in the story, narration, composition, etc. The topic marker は [*wa*], on the other hand, works like the definite article "the." The topic marker は [*wa*] replaces が [*ga*] when the subject has already been introduced or is known from the context. Once the subject becomes the topic, it may be deleted from following sentences when the meaning is clear. In fact, it is better and more natural not to repeat things that are understood from context or have already been mentioned.

Consider the following passage:

昔ある所に、もさくとみのきちという猟師の親子が住
んでいました。ある冬の日のこと、二人は山に猟に
出かけました。どんどん獲物を追って山の奥の方に
入ってゆくうちに、日が暮れて来ました。そして冷
たい風も吹き始めました。

*Mukashi aru tokoro ni Mosaku to Minokichi to iu ryōshi
no oyako ga sunde imashita. Aru fuyu no hi no koto, futari wa yama ni ryō ni dekakemashita. Dondon emono
o otte yama no oku no hō ni haitte yuku uchi ni, hi ga
kurete kimashita. Soshite tsumetai kaze mo fukihajime-
mashita.*

Translation: Once upon a time, at a certain place, there
lived two hunters named Mosaku and Minokichi, who
were father and son. One winter day, the two men went
out hunting. As they chased after game and went deep
into the mountains, the sun began to set and a cold
wind began to blow.

In the first sentence of this passage, が [*ga*] marks the subject, that is, the father-son hunters named Mosaku and Minokichi. In the second sentence, the topic marker は [*wa*]
replaces が [*ga*], because the subject—the two people—has
already been introduced. In the first half of the third sentence,
neither a topic nor a subject is mentioned, because it is clear
who is hunting.

Since the Japanese language tends not to repeat subjects
that have already been introduced or are understood from the
context, continued reference is seen as heavy-handed and unnecessary. This applies in particular to わたしは [*watashi
wa*] and わたしが [*watashi ga*], the overuse of which can
make the speaker seem excessively self-assertive.

As mentioned on page 18, the topic cannot be part of a
noun modifier. Consider the following examples:

(a) わたしは来た時にはいませんでした。
*Watashi wa kita toki ni wa imasen deshita.*

(b) わたしが来た時にはいませんでした。
*Watashi ga kita toki ni wa imasen deshita.*

In both of these sentences, 来た [*kita*] is a noun modifier that modifies 時 [*toki*]. Since わたし [*watashi*] in example (a) is marked by は [*wa*], it is the subject only of いませんでした [*imasen deshita*]. Thus (a) means "When he/she came, I was not there." In (b), the が [*ga*] marks わたし [*watashi*] as the subject of 来た [*kita*], so (b) means "When I came, he/she was not there."

In written text, a comma after the subject marker が [*ga*] is important. It indicates that the subject is not only for the following verb:

ごめんなさい。わたしが、きのう来た時に壊したんです。
*Gomen nasai. Watashi ga, kinō kita toki ni kowashita n' desu.*

I am sorry. I broke it when I came here yesterday. (I am the one who should be blamed.)

### ❖ Focus of Sentence

The choice between は [*wa*] and が [*ga*] can also shift the focus of a sentence. Consider the following:

(a) これは本です。　　*Kore wa hon desu.*
(b) これが本です。　　*Kore ga hon desu.*

What is the difference between (a) and (b)? Remember that in an A は [*wa*] B sentence the focus is on *what* or *how*, while in an A が [*ga*] B sentence the focus is on *which*. The sentence これは本です [*Kore wa hon desu*] indicates or defines what これ [*kore*] is (i.e., a book), while これが本です [*Kore ga hon desu*] indicates which of several things is the book or which is the book in question.

---

**Exercise 2** ————————————————————

Translate the following into Japanese.

1. Who are you?      I am [your name].
2. Which one is your book?    This one is mine.
3. Which one of you is [your name]?    I am [your name].
4. How is that book?      It (this book) is interesting.

---

### ➻ Focus of a Question

The focus of a question may change depending on whether は [*wa*] or が [*ga*] is used.

(a) あれは何ですか。      What's that?
     *Are wa nan desu ka.*

     （あれは）東京タワーです。    That's Tokyo Tower.
     *(Are wa) Tōkyō-tawā desu.*

(b) どれが歴史の本ですか。    Which is the history book?
     *Dore ga rekishi no hon desu ka.*

     これ（が歴史の本）です。    This is it.
     *Kore (ga rekishi no hon) desu.*

In (a), the main question is 何ですか [*nan desu ka*] "what." In other words, the speaker wants to identify an object that is located over there. Either the speaker is pointing at the tower or the listener knows what the speaker is referring to, so it is unnecessary to repeat それは [*sore wa*] in the answer. In (b), both the speaker and the listener know that a history book is among the many books in front of them. The speaker, however, does not know which one is the history book. The focus of the question is on "which," so in the answer it is unnecessary to mention that what they're looking for is a history book.

---

• Questions and Answers with は [*wa*] and が [*ga*]

If a question uses が [*ga*], the answer must also use が [*ga*]. If a question uses は [*wa*], the answer must follow suit. In other words, それは何ですか [*sore wa nan desu ka*] cannot be answered with これが本です [*kore ga hon desu*].

Some examples:

Q: あなた<u>は</u>どなたですか。
A: わたし<u>は</u>山田です。
*Q: Anata <u>wa</u> donata desu ka?*
*A: Watashi <u>wa</u> Yamada desu.*
Q: Who are you?
A: I'm Yamada.

Q: どれ<u>が</u>おたくの車ですか。
A: あれ<u>が</u>うちのです。
*Q: Dore <u>ga</u> otaku no kuruma desu ka?*
*A: Are <u>ga</u> uchi no desu.*
Q: Which car is yours?
A: That one is ours.

---

## ❖ Position of も [*mo*]

The English sentence "I'll go to Kyoto, too" is ambiguous in isolation because "too" may refer to either "I" or "Kyoto."

Japanese is less vague here, because も [*mo*] "too" immediately follows the word it refers to.

Compare the following:

わたし<u>も</u>京都に行きます。

*Watashi <u>mo</u> Kyōto ni ikimasu.*

I, as well as others, will go to Kyoto.

わたしは京都に<u>も</u>行きます。

*Watashi wa Kyōto ni <u>mo</u> ikimasu.*

I will go to Kyoto as well as to other places.

---

- Questions and Answers with も [*mo*]

If the question has も [*mo*] and the answer is affirmative (namely "yes"), answer with も [*mo*]. If the question has も [*mo*], and the answer is negative (namely "no"), answer with は [*wa*]. For example:

Q: これは何ですか。

A: それはペンです。

Q: じゃあ、これ<u>も</u>ペンですか。

A: いいえ、それ<u>は</u>ペンじゃありません。*or* はい、それ<u>も</u>ペンです。

*Q: Kore wa nan desu ka.*

*A: Sore wa pen desu.*

*Q: Jā, kore <u>mo</u> pen desu ka.*

*A: Iie, sore <u>wa</u> pen ja arimasen.* or *Hai, sore <u>mo</u> pen desu.*

Q: What is this?

A: This is a pen.

Q: Well, is this a pen, too?

A: No, that is not a pen. *or* Yes, that's a pen, too.

---

## ➥ Additional Information

The topic marker は [*wa*] may be used to indicate that the speaker has in mind a contrast or is suggesting additional information. For example:

(a) 来年、ヨーロッパに行く。
*Rainen, Yōroppa ni iku.*

(b) 来年は、ヨーロッパに行く。
*Rainen wa, Yōroppa ni iku.*

(c) ヨーロッパには行く。
*Yōroppa ni wa iku.*

Sentence (a) simply says that the speaker is planning to go to Europe next year. Sentence (b) suggests additional information, such as that the speaker went to some other place this year or that circumstances did not allow him to go to Europe this year but that he still hopes to go next year. Sentence (c) may mean, "I'll go at least to Europe (even if I cannot go other places)." In (b), the は [*wa*] with 来年 [*rainen*] shows the contrast with other years, while in (c) the は [*wa*] with ヨーロッパに [*Yōroppa ni*] shows a contrast with other places to visit.

## ➥ Negation

The topic marker は [*wa*] is also used with some patterns to partially negate a previous statement or idea. Some examples:

> Q: どうして行かないの？疲れてるの？
> A: 疲れてはいないけど、今夜は寒いから出かけたくない。

> *Q: Dōshite ikanai no? Tsukarete 'ru no?*
> *A: Tsukarete <u>wa</u> inai kedo, kon'ya wa samui kara dekake-taku nai.*

Q: Why aren't you going? Are you tired?

A: It's not that I am tired, but it's cold tonight so I don't want to go out.

Q: 高いから買わないの？

A: 高く<u>は</u>ないけど、色が嫌いだから……。

*Q: Takai kara kawanai no?*

*A: Takaku <u>wa</u> nai kedo, iro ga kirai da kara …*

Q: So you aren't going to buy it because it's expensive?

A: It's not that it's expensive. I just don't like the color …

Q: そんな派手なドレス、買うの？

A: 買い<u>は</u>しないけど、ちょっと着てだけみようかと思って。

*Q: Sonna hade na doresu, kau no?*

*A: Kai <u>wa</u> shinai kedo, chotto kite dake miyō ka to omotte.*

Q: Are you really going to buy such a gaudy dress?

A: I don't intend to buy it, but I thought I would at least try it on.

---

### Exercise 3 —————————————

Translate the following into English.

1. 遅くても三時までには来て下さいよ。
   *Osokute mo sanji made ni wa kite kudasai yo.*
2. ペンは買ったけど、シャープペンは買わなかった。
   *Pen wa katta kedo, shāpupen wa kawanakatta.*
3. 忙しくても、あの人には会って来ようと思う。
   *Isogashikute mo, ano hito ni wa atte koyō to omou.*
4. 雨が降ってはいるけど、傘が要るほどじゃない。
   *Ame ga futte wa iru kedo, kasa ga iru hodo ja nai.*
5. あの人に会ったことはあるけど名前は知らない。
   *Ano hito ni atta koto wa aru kedo namae wa shiranai.*

## ❖❖ With Interrogatives

With an interrogative word (such as 何 [*nani*] "what" or どこ [*doko*] "where"), there's a simple rule for choosing between は [*wa*] and が [*ga*]: use は [*wa*] before an interrogative and が [*ga*] after. Some examples:

Q: これは何ですか。
A: ペンです。
*Q: Kore wa nan desu ka.*
*A: Pen desu.*
Q: What is this?
A: This is a pen.

Q: そこはどこですか。
A: タカノの前です。
*Q: Soko wa doko desu ka.*
*A: Takano no mae desu.*
Q: Where is it (that place)?
A: It is in front of Takano's.

Q: 昨日あなたといた人は誰ですか。
A: 娘です。
*Q: Sakujitsu anata to ita hito wa dare desu ka.*
*A: Musume desu.*
Q: Who was the person with you yesterday?
A: It was my daughter.

Q: 誰が来たのですか。
A: 山本さんです。
*Q: Dare ga kita no desu ka.*
*A: Yamamoto-san desu.*
Q: Who came?
A: Mr. Yamamoto.

Q: どこのが一番おいしいですか。

A: ヤナギでしょう。

*Q: Doko no ga ichiban oishii desu ka.*

*A: Yanagi deshō.*

Q: Which place has the best food?

A: Probably Yanagi's.

Q: 何が要るのですか。

A: はさみです。

*Q: Nani ga iru no desu ka.*

*A: Hasami desu.*

Q: What do you need?

A: I need some scissors.

## ■ こ-そ-あ-ど [ko-so-a-do] Words

The こ-そ-あ-ど [ko-so-a-do] words are demonstratives such as ここ [koko], そちら [sochira], あの [ano], どれ [dore], etc. When these words refer to objects that are visible to the speaker and hearer, they are similar to demonstratives such as "this" and "that" in English. For example, これ [kore] means "this thing," while それ [sore] means "that thing (near you)" and あれ [are] means "that thing (over there)."

When the words refer to things that are not seen or directly experienced, they sometimes become troublesome. Especially in reading, one must be careful with the meaning of こ-そ-あ-ど [ko-so-a-do] words. This section focuses on when these words refer to unseen entities such as experience, knowledge, or ideas. In such contexts, these four prefixes have the following meanings:

こ [ko]: refers to a present matter known by both speaker and listener

そ [so]: excludes the speaker; refers to a previously mentioned matter, statement, etc.

あ [*a*]: excludes the listener; refers to past experience, knowledge, etc. shared by both speaker and listener

ど [*do*]: indicates the interrogative forms

When こ - [*ko-*] and そ - [*so-*] refer to ideas, statements, thoughts, etc., こ - [*ko-*] refers either to what was just mentioned or to what will be mentioned soon after, while そ - [*so-*] refers only to something that has been mentioned before.

Some examples:

(a) <u>この</u>映画、ちっとも面白くないわね。Ⓕ
<u>*Kono*</u> *eiga, chittomo omoshiroku nai wa ne.*
This movie isn't at all interesting, is it.

(b) <u>それ</u>、いつの話？
<u>*Sore*</u>, *itsu no hanashi?*
When did that (thing you have been talking about) happen?

(c) 週末に東北の温泉に行ってきたのですけれど、<u>あそこ</u>はまだ雪でしたよ。
*Shūmatsu ni Tōhoku no onsen ni itte kita no desu keredo,*
<u>*asoko*</u> *wa mada yuki deshita yo.*
I went to a hot spring in Tōhoku; it was still snowing there.

(d) ゆうべのラーメンおいしかった。また<u>あそこ</u>に行こうよ。
*Yūbe no rāmen oishikatta. Mata* <u>*asoko*</u> *ni ikō yo.*
The ramen (that we ate) last night was very good. Let's go there again.

In (a), both the speaker and listener are watching a movie, so the knowledge about which movie is shared by both. In (b), それ [*sore*] suggests that the speaker was not a part of the happening or incident. In other words, it is only in the other person's memory. The あそこ [*asoko*] in (c) refers to a place that only the speaker visited. That is, the listener did not participate in the visit to the hot spring that the speaker is discussing. In (d), the speaker and the listener share the same memory: they went to eat ramen together.

Here are some more examples of こ-そ-あ-ど [ko-so-a-do].

山田： 昨夜お宅にお電話したのですけれどちょうどお留守だったようですね。

ジョナソン： そうでしたか。<u>それは</u>すみませんでした。

*Yamada:* *Sakuya otaku ni odenwa shita no desu keredo chōdo orusu datta yō desu ne.*

*Jonason:* *Sō deshita ka. <u>Sore wa</u> sumimasen deshita.*

Yamada: I called you last night. It seems that you were not at home.

Jonathan: You did? Sorry about that.

検事： あなたはこの写真の人物を見たことがありますか。

証人： はい。あります。

検事： <u>それは</u>いつのことでしたか。

証人： <u>あれは</u>昨年の夏のことだったと思います。

*Kenji:* *Anata wa kono shashin no jinbutsu o mita koto ga arimasu ka.*

*Shōnin:* *Hai. Arimasu.*

*Kenji:* *<u>Sore wa</u> itsu no koto deshita ka.*

*Shōnin:* *<u>Are wa</u> sakunen no natsu no koto datta to omoimasu.*

Prosecutor: Have you ever seen the person in this picture?

Witness: Yes, I have.

Prosecutor: When was that?

Witness: I think that it was last summer.

今度大阪にもドームが出来るそうですが、<u>そこ</u>から近いのですか。一緒に東京ドームで巨人戦を見た時、<u>あそこ</u>の大きいことにびっくりしましたが、大阪ドームはもっと大きいとか、楽しみですね。

*Kondo Ōsaka ni mo dōmu ga dekiru sō desu ga, <u>soko</u> kara chikai no desu ka. Issho ni Tōkyō-dōmu de Kyojin-sen o mita toki, <u>asoko</u> no ōkii koto ni bikkuri shimashita ga, Ōsaka-dōmu wa motto ōkii to ka, tanoshimi desu ne.*

I heard that they are now building a dome in Osaka, too. Is your place near there? When we saw the Giants game in Tokyo Dome together, I was surprised at the size of the dome, but they say that the Osaka Dome will be much bigger. Isn't that exciting?

## ■ Locatives

Explanations of location or direction are sometimes confusing because Japanese sentence structure is different from that of English. Compare the following:

(a) <u>わたしの</u> <u>うちの</u> <u>となりに</u> <u>教会が</u> <u>あります</u>。
    1       2      3     4    5
<u>Watashi no</u> <u>uchi no</u> <u>tonari ni</u> <u>kyōkai ga</u> <u>arimasu</u>.
<u>There is</u> <u>a church</u> <u>next to</u> <u>my</u> <u>house</u>.
   5      4      3    1    2

(b) <u>わたしの</u> <u>うちの</u> <u>となりは</u> <u>教会</u> です。
    1       2      3     4  5
<u>Watashi no</u> <u>uchi no</u> <u>tonari wa</u> <u>kyōkai</u> desu.
<u>Next to</u> <u>my</u> <u>house</u> <u>is</u> <u>a church</u>.
   3      1      2    5    4

(c) <u>教会は</u> <u>わたしの</u> <u>うちの</u> <u>となり</u> です。
    1      2      3    4  5
<u>Kyōkai wa</u> <u>watashi no</u> <u>uchi no</u> <u>tonari</u> <u>desu</u>.

<u>The church</u> <u>is</u> <u>next to</u> <u>my</u> <u>house</u>.
  1        5   4    2    3

(d) <u>それは</u> <u>わたしの</u> <u>うちの</u> <u>となりの</u> <u>教会</u> <u>です</u>。
   1      2       3       4     5   6

<u>*Sore wa* *watashi no* *uchi no* *tonari no* *kyōkai* *desu*</u>.
<u>That one</u> <u>is</u> <u>the church</u> <u>next to</u> <u>my</u> <u>house</u>.
  1      6      5        4   2   3

Sentence (a) tells what is located next to my house; (b) tells what the neighboring building is; (c) tells the location of a particular church; and (d) tells which one is the church under discussion.

Sentences (c) and (d) are the "A is B" type, so it is not correct to say 教会はわたしのうちのとなり<u>に</u>です [*Kyōkai wa watashi no uchi no tonari ni desu*] or それはわたしのうちのとなり<u>に</u>教会です [*Sore wa watashi no uchi no tonari ni kyōkai desu*]. In sentence (c), the です [*desu*] replaces に あります [*ni arimasu*].

---

### *Exercise 4* ───────────────

For each of the sentences above, write a question that would be answered by that sentence.

    (a) _____
    (b) _____
    (c) _____
    (d) _____

# CONNECTING WORDS

This chapter focuses on how elements of Japanese sentences are linked together. In English, the conjunction "and" can connect nouns to nouns and verbs to verbs in most contexts, but in Japanese the connecting word varies depending on the type of elements being linked as well as the shades of meaning.

## ■ Connecting Nouns or Noun Phrases ─────

### ●● Listing Things, Names, etc.

◇ *Exhaustive Listing:* と [*to*]

The conjunction と [*to*] is used to connect series of nouns that are exhaustive. In other words, the words linked by と [*to*] are the complete list and there are no others.

Some examples:

A: 机の上に何がありますか。
B: 本とノートとペンがあります／です。
A: *Tsukue no ue ni nani ga arimasu ka.*
B: *Hon to nōto to pen ga arimasu / desu.*
A: What is on the desk?
B: There are books, notebooks, and pens (and that's all).

Students of Japanese often connect sentences like わたしは東京に行きます [*Watashi wa Tokyo ni ikimasu*] and 銀座で買物をします [*Ginza de kaimono o shimasu*] with the particle と [*to*]. This common mistake seems to come about because the students think that と [*to*] is the same as "and" in all usages. Remember that と [*to*] is used only between nouns.

✧ *Partial Listing:* や [*ya*], とか [*to ka*]

When a list of nouns is not exhaustive, they can be connected by the particles や [*ya*] or とか [*to ka*]. For example:

(a) 本<u>や</u>ノートがあります。
　　*Hon <u>ya</u> nōto ga arimasu.*
　　There are books, notebooks, and other things.

(b) ジーン<u>とか</u>マリー<u>とか</u>……あとは誰が居たか覚えていないんです。
　　*Jīn <u>to ka</u> Marī <u>to ka</u> ... ato wa dare ga ita ka oboete inai n' desu.*
　　Jean and Marie and ... I don't remember who else was there besides them.

In example (a), the speaker is simply not mentioning the whole list, perhaps because there are too many things to list or the speaker is busy or lazy. Thus the particle や [*ya*] is used to name or list a part of the whole.

As shown in (b), とか [*to ka*] may be used interchangeably with や [*ya*]. Sometimes, though, とか [*to ka*] may also show the speaker's reluctance or uncertainty. In the following example, the speaker hesitates to give a full listing because she wants to hide something.

刑事：　　　そこに誰がいたんだ？みんないたのか？Ⓜ
容疑者Ａ：　ジーン<u>とか</u>マリー<u>とか</u>……。あとは誰がいたか覚えていないんです。

*Keiji:*　　　*Soko ni dare ga ita n' da? Minna ita no ka?*

*Yōgisha A:*　*Jīn <u>to ka</u> Marī <u>to ka</u> ... Ato wa dare ga ita ka oboete inai n' desu.*

Detective:　Who was there? Was everybody there?

Suspect A:  Jean and Marie and ... I don't remember who else was there besides them.

Like と [*to*], the particle や [*ya*] is used only with nouns and noun phrases. However, と か [*to ka*] may also occur with verbs or verb phrases, as shown by the following example:

テリー：　お休み、何してたの？
恵子：　　買物をする<u>とか</u>映画を見に行く<u>とか</u>……。
　　　　　でも一週間なんて、すぐ過ぎてしまうものね。

*Terī:*　*Oyasumi, nani shite 'ta no?*
*Keiko:*　*Kaimono o suru <u>to ka</u> eiga o mi ni iku <u>to ka</u> ...*
　　　　*Demo isshūkan nante, sugu sugite shimau mono*
　　　　*ne.*

Terry:　What did you do during your vacation?
Keiko:　I went shopping and went to the movies and (I did other things like that) ... Anyway, one week passes much too quickly.

The particle など [*nado*] often occurs with や [*ya*] or と か [*to ka*] without changing the meaning, as in the following sentence:

セーター<u>や／とか</u>ハンドバッグ<u>や／とか</u>イアリング
（など）を買った。

*Sētā <u>ya/to ka</u> hando-baggu <u>ya/to ka</u> iaringu (nado) o katta.*
I bought things like a sweater, a handbag, and a pair of earrings.

◇ *Selective Listing:* か [*ka*], なり [*nari*]

The particles か [*ka*] and なり [*nari*] may be used interchangeably to indicate "or." However, なり [*nari*] usually indicates a selection from a category of two or more specific items while か [ka] may simply list a suggestion from a random group of items.

(a) 今夜か／なり明日か／なり、お電話ください。

*Kon'ya ka/nari asu ka/nari, odenwa kudasai.*

Please call me tonight or tomorrow.

(b) 夏休みには、ニュージーランドかオーストラリアか（どこか）に行くつもりです。

*Natsu-yasumi ni wa, Nyūjīrando ka Ōsutoraria ka (doko ka) ni iku tsumori desu.*

I'm planning to go somewhere like New Zealand or Australia (or someplace else) during summer vacation.

(c) ペンなり万年筆なり、お好きな方をお取り下さい。

*Pen nari mannen-hitsu nari, osuki na hō o otori kudasai.*

Please take a pen or a fountain pen, whichever you prefer.

In sentence (a), the choice is specific, so か [ka] is interchangeable with なり [nari]. In (b), though, it is better to use か [ka] because it is merely a random list. In (c), なり [nari] is the most appropriate because it indicates a choice from a category of two specific items.

---

- Formal Connections

In formal speech or writing, the following expressions may be used instead of the particles mentioned above.

氏名、並びに住所をお書き下さい。

*Shimei, narabi ni jūsho o okaki kudasai.*

Please write your name and address.

姓名及び生年月日を記入すること。

*Seimei oyobi seinen-gappi o kinyū suru koto.*

Fill in your name and date of birth.

来年、又は再来年、開店す予定でおります。

*Rainen, <u>mata wa</u> sarainen, kaiten suru yotei de orimasu.*

We are planning to open the store next year or the year
after next.

十日までに電話、あるいは、書簡でご返答ください。

*Tōka made ni denwa, <u>aruiwa</u>, shokan de gohentō kuda-
sai.*

Please respond by telephone or letter by the tenth.

•• **Conversational Connectors:** そして [*soshite*], それから
[*sore kara*]

When listing things and names in conversation, the conjunctive そして [*soshite*] or それから [*sore kara*] may also
be used. Some examples:

(a) 花子：　夕べの同級会でどんな物が出たの？
　　ジョー：あのね、飲み物とおすしとそうめんサラダ
　　　　　　とパスタサラダと<u>そして</u>……。何だっけ、
　　　　　　忘れちゃった。

*Hanako:*　*Yūbe no dōkyū-kai de donna mono ga deta no?*
*Jō:*　　　*Ano ne, nomimono to osushi to sōmen-sarada
to pasuta-sarada to <u>soshite</u> … Nan dakke, wasu-
rechatta.*

Hanako:　What was served at last night's class reunion?
Joe:　　　Well, drinks, sushi, sōmen salad, pasta salad,
and … What was it? I forget.

(b) ジョー：アメリカの西海岸ではどこに行ったの？
　　花子：　サンフランシスコ、ロングビーチ、<u>それか
　　　　　　ら</u>サンタクルーズ。

*Jō:*       *America no nishi-kaigan de wa doko ni itta no?*
*Hanako:*   *Sanfuranshisuko, Longubīchi, <u>sore kara</u> Santa-*
            *kurūzu.*
Joe:        Where did you go on the West Coast of the
            U.S.?
Hanako:     San Francisco, Long Beach, and Santa Cruz.

そして [*soshite*] and それから [*sore kara*] are often inter-changeable, but それから [*sore kara*] usually lists items in sequential order, as shown in (b).

# ■ Connecting Verbs or Verb Phrases

The particle と [*to*] is used only to connect nouns or noun phrases. It cannot link clauses or sentences. Thus sentences like 雪がふりましたとさむかったです [*Yuki ga furimashita <u>to</u> samukatta desu.* It snowed and was cold], though often heard in the speech of beginning students, are incorrect.

The most common patterns for linking verbs and verb phrases use the -て [*-te*] form of the verb.

## ❧ Listing Sequential or Concurrent Actions, Events, etc.

The basic function of the -て [*-te*] form is to connect verbs or verb phrases. In this pattern (A -て [*-te*] B), the action or event represented by A usually precedes B in time, though in some cases A and B are concurrent.

(a) 正子は家族のために<u>夕食の仕度をして</u> <u>出かけた</u>。
                              A            B

*Masako wa kazoku no tame ni <u>yūshoku no shitaku o shite</u>*
*<u>dekaketa</u>.*

Masako prepared dinner for her family and (then) went out.

(b) ケンは<u>コーヒーを飲んで</u> <u>サンドイッチを食べた</u>。
        A                        B

*Ken wa <u>kōhī o nonde</u> <u>sandoitchi o tabeta</u>.*
Ken drank coffee and ate a sandwich.

In example (a), Masako did the two things sequentially, while in (b) Ken did the two things concurrently.

---

- Notes on -て Form

(1) The A -て [-*te*] B pattern cannot be reversed. That is, B never precedes A.

(2) The -て [-*te*] form of だ／です [*da/desu*] is -で [-*de*], the -て [-*te*] form of -である [-*de aru*] is -であって [-*de atte*], and the -て [-*te*] form of adjectives is -くて [-*kute*].

これは日本の話<u>で</u>、「桃太郎」といいます。
*Kore wa Nihon no hanashi <u>de</u>, "Momotarō" to iimasu.*
This is a Japanese tale, and it is called "Momotarō."

この部屋は静か<u>で</u>眺めもいい。
*Kono heya wa shizuka <u>de</u> nagame mo ii.*
This room is quiet and has a nice view.

わたしの部屋は広<u>くて</u>涼しい。
*Watashi no heya wa hiro<u>kute</u> suzushii.*
My room is spacious and cool.

今回のことは基地問題にも関するもの<u>であって</u>, 単なる犯罪として扱うべきではない。
*Konkai no koto wa kichi-mondai ni mo kansuru mono <u>de atte</u>, tannaru hanzai toshite atsukau beki de wa nai.*
This incident is also related to the base issue, so it should not be handled just as a crime.

---

The stem of the -ます [-*masu*] form is used to connect verbs and verb phrases in formal speech and writing.

The next example is from a news broadcast:

昨夜、上越地方に大雪が<u>降り</u>、新幹線が不通になりました。

*Sakuya, Jōetsu-chihō ni ōyuki ga <u>furi</u>, Shinkan-sen ga futsū ni narimashita.*

Last night, heavy snow fell in the Jōetsu area, and the Shinkansen (bullet train) was halted.

---

• Stem of -ます [-*masu*] Form of いる [*iru*]

The -ます [-*masu*] form of いる [*iru*] "to exist" is います [i*masu*], so the stem of its -ます [-*masu*] form is い- [*i-*]. However, おり- [ori-] is more commonly used. This おり- [ori-] is derived from the verb おる [oru], which is the humble form of いる [iru]. When -ており [-*te ori*] is used to connect verbs or verb phrases, though, it does not express any humility.

残念なことに、友達は出かけて<u>おり</u>、会うことが出来ませんでした。

*Zannen na koto ni, tomodachi wa dekakete <u>ori</u>, au koto ga dekimasen deshita.*

Unfortunately, my friend was not at home, and (so) I could not see him.

---

## ❧ Restrictions on the -て [-*te*] Form

The basic function of the -て [-*te*] form is to connect two sentences that describe successive or concurrent events, actions, etc., so it is not appropriate to use -て [-*te*] form when the two sentences are not related. Nor can you use the -て [-*te*] form to link two statements when one of the statements is stative and the other indicates action, motion, etc. except when the first sentence explains the direct cause for the second.

The following examples are correct:

頭が痛くて起きられなかった。

*Atama ga itakute okirarenakatta.*

I had a headache, and so I couldn't get up.

合格を知った時には嬉しくて跳び上がってしまった。

*Gōkaku o shitta toki ni wa ureshikute tobiagatte shimatta.*

When I learned that I'd passed the exams, I jumped for joy.

希望の会社から採用通知をもらってとても嬉しかった。

*Kibō no kaisha kara saiyō-tsūchi o moratte totemo ureshi-katta.*

I received notice of employment from the company where I hoped to work, so I was very happy.

The next three examples not acceptable:

(a) 卒業したら仕事を探したいと思って、そのすぐ後で結婚するつもりです。

*Sotsugyō shitara shigoto o sagashitai to omotte, sono sugu ato de kekkon suru tsumori desu.*

I am thinking of looking for a job when I graduate, and soon after that I intend to get married.

(b) 日本のテレビ番組を見て、興味があった。

*Nihon no terebi-bangumi o mite, kyōmi ga atta.*

I watched some Japanese TV programs, and I found them interesting.

(c) 安くて買いたい。

*Yasukute kaitai.*

It's inexpensive, and I want to buy it.

Sentence (a) is incorrect because there is no cause-and-effect relation between the two clauses linked by the -て [-te] form. An appropriate sentence might be 卒業したらすぐ仕事を探して、(見つかったら)その後で結婚するつもりです [Sotsugyō shitara sugu shigoto o sagashite, (mitsukattara) sono ato de kekkon suru tsumori desu.] "Soon after I'll graduate I'm going to look for a job; (if I find one) then I intend to get married." In this case, finding a job is a prerequisite to the speaker getting married.

Sentences (b) and (c) are incorrect because one of the clauses is stative (興味があった [kyōmi ga atta] and 安くて [yasukute]) while the other uses an action verb (日本のテレビ番組を見て [Nihon no terebi-bangumi o mite] and 買いたい [kaitai]). In addition, the first clause is not perceived as the direct cause of the second. The correct sentences might be 日本のテレビ番組を見て興味がわいてきた [Nihon no terebi-bangumi o mite kyōmi ga waite kita] "I watched some Japanese TV programs and they aroused my interest" and 安いから／安いので買いたい [yasui kara / yasui no de kaitai] "I want to buy it because it is inexpensive."

## ➡ Idiomatic Usages of the -て [-te] Form

The -て [-te] form may be used with another verb to indicate additional information, describe emotions, etc.

### ✧ A -て [-te] B

The -て [-te] form may indicate a reason, cause, excuse, etc. for the statement *immediately* following. Therefore, in the following example 風邪をひいて [kaze o hiite] is the reason for 熱があります [netsu ga arimasu] but not for 休ませました [yasumasemashita]. The compound clause 風邪をひいて熱がある [kaze o hiite netsu ga aru] states why the speaker made her son miss school.

息子は、風邪をひいて熱があるので休ませました。

*Musuko wa, kaze o hiite netsu ga aru no de yasumase-mashita.*

My son had a fever because he had caught a cold, so I made him stay home.

The -て [-*te*] form in the A -て [-*te*] B pattern describes a reason, cause, etc., but only implicitly, not directly. The -て [-*te*] form suggests that A is the reason for B, while から [*kara*], ので [*no de*], ために [*tame ni*], and もので [*mono de*] explicitly specify the reason for B.

(a) 昨夜は友人が<u>来て</u>出かけられませんでした。

*Sakuya wa yūjin ga <u>kite</u> dekakeraremasen deshita.*

Last night, a friend came to visit me and (so) I was unable to go out.

(b) 昨夜は友人が来た<u>から</u>／<u>ので</u>／<u>ために</u>／<u>もので</u>出かけられませんでした。

*Sakuya wa yūjin ga kita <u>kara</u> / <u>no de</u> / <u>tame ni</u> / <u>mono de</u> dekakeraremasen deshita.*

Because a friend came to see me last night, I was unable to go out.

Example (a) with -て [-*te*] is less direct, so it sounds softer and less assertive. Example (b) may imply that the speaker is trying to avoid taking blame by putting responsibility on his friend rather than himself.

✧ -ていく [-*te iku*]／-てくる [-*te kuru*]

The verbs いく [*iku*] and くる [*kuru*] after the -て [-*te*] form indicate the direction of the action or motion expressed by the preceding verb. Some examples:

持っていく [*motte iku*]     to take (of inanimate objects)

持って来る [*motte kuru*]    to bring (of inanimate objects)
連れて行く [*tsurete iku*]    to take (of animate objects)
連れて来る [*tsurete kuru*]  to bring (of animate objects)

The phrase 持って行く [*motte iku*] literally means "to hold and go," while 持って来る [*motte kuru*] means "to hold and come," while 連れて行く [*tsurete iku*] and 連れて来る [*tsurete kuru*] mean "to take along and go" and "to take along and come." In Japanese, the -て来る [*-te kuru*] and -て行く [*-te iku*] endings function similarly to the English adverbs "in" and "out."

Compare the following:

部屋に入って来た。
*Heya ni haitte kita.*
He came into the room.
(I.e., he entered the room and came towards the speaker.)

部屋に入って行った。
*Heya ni haitte itta.*
He went into the room.
(I.e., he entered the room and went away from the speaker.)

Here are some more examples of the -て来る [*-te kuru*] and -て行く [*-te iku*] endings:

雨が降りそうだから、かさを持って行きなさい。
*Ame ga furisō da kara, kasa o motte ikinasai.*
It looks like it's going to rain, so take your umbrella with you.

来る時そこの机の上の本、持って来て！
*Kuru toki soko no tsukue no ue no hon, motte kite!*
Bring the book on the desk for me when you come!

あした、子供たちを動物園に連れて行きます。

*Ashita, kodomo-tachi o dōbutsu-en ni tsurete ikimasu.*
I'm taking the children to the zoo tomorrow.

あすのパーティーに友人を連れて来てもいいですか。
*Asu no pātī ni yūjin o tsurete kite mo ii desu ka.*
May I bring a friend to the party tomorrow?

小鳥が飛んできて庭の木にとまった。でもすぐ飛んで
行ってしまった。
*Kotori ga tonde kite niwa no ki ni tomatta. Demo sugu
tonde itte shimatta.*
A small bird flew in and perched in a tree in our yard. But
it soon flew away.

In English, it is quite natural to say "I'm going out to eat"
without adding "and then I'll come back," since it is clearly
understood that the speaker will return. The opposite is the
case in Japanese, where the emphasis is placed on the coming
back. Instead, it is the going that is taken as understood. For
example:

僕は食べてくるから晩ご飯はいらない。Ⓜ
*Boku wa tabete kuru kara ban-gohan wa iranai.*
I'll eat out, so I won't need supper.
(Lit., I'll eat and come (back), so I don't need supper.)

もうすぐ夕飯が出きるから、食べていったら。
*Mō sugu yūhan ga dekiru kara, tabete ittara.*
Supper will soon be ready, so why don't you eat with us
(before you go).

### ●● -ていく／-てくる [*-te iku/-te kuru*] with **Momentary Verbs**

When the -て [*-te*] form is a momentary verb, it indicates that
a change will occur or that an action or motion will begin.

For example:

突然、雨が降ってきた。
*Totsuzen, ame ga futte kita.*
Suddenly it started to rain.

夕暮れになると谷底から霧が立ってくる。
*Yūgure ni naru to tanizoko kara kiri ga tatte kuru.*
At twilight, the mist begins to rise from the bottom of the
   valley.

---

* Examples of Momentary Verbs

**Transition from One State to Another**

| | |
|---|---|
| 知る [*shiru*] | to realize |
| 壊れる [*kowareru*] | to break apart |
| 死ぬ [*shinu*] | to die |
| 入る [*hairu*] | to enter |
| 閉る [*tojiru*] | to close |
| 咲く [*saku*] | to bloom |
| 空く [*aku*] | to become vacant |

**Start of Action or Motion from Static State**

| | |
|---|---|
| 散る [*chiru*] | to fall, scatter (as of flower petals) |
| 倒れる [*taoreru*] | to fall over |
| 立つ [*tatsu*] | to stand up |
| 落ちる [*ochiru*] | to fall (from a height) |

**Arrival or Completion**

| | |
|---|---|
| 着く [*tsuku*] | to arrive (at a destination) |
| 届く [*todoku*] | to reach, to be delivered |
| 触れる [*fureru*] | to touch |

---

## ➻ Movement in Time

いく [*iku*] and くる [*kuru*] may also suggest movement in time: from the past towards the present, or from the present towards the future.

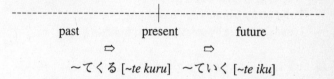

The choice between いく [*iku*] and くる [*kuru*] may also vary depending on the speaker's psychological or emotional involvement in the matter. Statements with -ていく [*-te iku*] are usually more objective. For instance, sentence (a) below is a statement based on an observation, while (b) shows the speaker's concern and anxiety.

(a) この町の人口はますます増えていくだろう。

*Kono machi no jinkō wa masumasu fuete iku darō.*

The population of this town will probably keep increasing.

(b) この町の車の数がこれ以上増えてくると大変だ。

*Kono machi no kuruma no kazu ga kore ijō fuete kuru to taihen da.*

There will be problems if the number of cars in this town increases any more.

## ➻ Manner of Action

The -て [*-te*] form may indicate how a motion, action, or movement occurs. In sentence (a) below, 電車に乗って [*densha ni notte*] tells how the speaker traveled, while in (b) ヤシの葉をあんで [*yashi no ha o ande*] tells how the speaker made the basket.

(a) 電車に乗って行った。

*Densha ni notte itta.*

I went by train. (Lit., I went by riding on a train.)

(b) ヤシの葉をあんで籠を作った。

*Yashi no ha o ande kago o tsukutta.*

I made a basket by weaving palm fronds.

### ✧ -ている [*-te iru*]／-てある[*-te aru*]

When non-native speakers of Japanese are asked 結婚していますか [*kekkon shite imasu ka*] "Are you married?," they often answer いいえ、結婚しません [*Iie, kekkon shimasen*], intending to say "No, I'm not married." However, 結婚しません [*kekkon shimasen*] does not have this meaning; instead, it means "I will not get married." Two appropriate answers to the question would be いいえ、結婚していません [*Iie, kekkon shite imasen*] "No, I am not married" and はい、結婚しています [*Hai, kekkon shite imasu*] "Yes, I am married."

In English, "I work at the Bank of Tokyo" and "I am working at the Bank of Tokyo" are nearly interchangeable. In Japanese, though, 東京銀行で働きます [*Tōkyō-ginkō de hatarakimasu*] and 東京銀行で働いています [*Tōkyō-ginkō de hataraite imasu*] have very different meanings. The former sentence says that the speaker will work at the Bank of Tokyo at some point in the future, while the latter says that the speaker is working at the bank now.

### ✧ -ている [*-te iru*]

When attached to the -て [*-te*] form of transitive verbs, the verb いる [*iru*] "to be, exist (of animate objects)" usually shows that something is in progress or that it occurs as part of a regular routine. When いる [*iru*] is appended to the -て [-*te*] form of intransitive or momentary verbs, though, it indicates a constant state that is the consequence of a past occurrence. This usage of -ている [-*te iru*] is possible only when the consequence is known or visible to the speaker.

Some examples:

(a) ケイが本を読んでいる。
*Kei ga hon o yonde iru.*
Kay is reading a book.

(b) お宅ではどんな新聞を読んでいますか。
*Otaku de wa donna shinbun o yonde imasu ka.*
Which newspaper do you read?

(c) 戸が閉っていて入れない。
*To ga shimatte ite hairenai.*
The door is closed, so I cannot enter.

(d) 水槽の魚が死んでいる。
*Suisō no sakana ga shinde iru.*
The fish in the tank is dead.

In (a), -ている [-*te iru*] indicates that the action of reading is in progress, while in (b) the speaker is asking what newspaper the other person reads daily, not what that person is doing right now. Example (c) describes the consequence of an event that has happened in the past (i.e., the closing of the door). In (d), the speaker's message is that the fish is dead and the dead body of the fish is still in the water tank.

The verb ending -た [-*ta*] refers only to what happened or what the subject did in the past, while -ている [-*te iru*] refers to a state that exists as a consequence of something earlier. For example:

父はゴルフに行きました。
*Chichi wa gorufu ni ikimashita.*
My father went to play golf.

| 父親の友人： | もしもし。お父さん、居る？ |
| 娘： | いいえ、父はゴルフに行ってい |
| | ます。 |

*Chichioya no yūjin:*     *Moshimoshi. Otōsan, iru?*
*Musume:*     *Iie, Chichi wa gorufu ni itte imasu.*
Father's friend:     Hello. Is your father there?
Daughter:     No, he has gone to play golf.

In this example, the daughter is emphasizing that her father is not at home.

The ending -ている [-*te iru*] may be used with a transitive verb to indicate an event that occurred in the past but still has consequences in the present:

その年、芥川は「蜘蛛の糸」を書いている。
*Sono toshi, Akutagawa wa "Kumo no Ito" o kaite iru.*
In that year, Akutagawa wrote "Kumo no Ito" (and it is still read by people today).

---

### Exercise 5

For each of the following sentences, identify whether the meaning of the -ている [-*te iru*] form is progressive, routine, or resultative.

Example:

母はいま台所で食事の仕度を<u>しています</u>。
*Haha wa ima daidokoro de shokuji no shitaku o <u>shite imasu</u>.*

---

Answer: Progressive

1. 健康のために毎日一時間ぐらい<u>歩いています</u>。
   *Kenkō no tame ni mainichi ichijikan gurai <u>aruite imasu</u>.*

2. 父は貿易会社に<u>勤めています</u>。
   *Chichi wa bōeki-gaisha ni <u>tsutomete imasu</u>.*

3. 山田君、<u>来ている</u>?
   *Yamada-kun, <u>kite iru</u>?*

4. わたしたちは一ヶ月に一度は集まって情報を交換<u>し合っています</u>。
   *Watashi-tachi wa ikkagetsu ni ichido wa atsumatte jōhō o kōkan <u>shiatte imasu</u>.*

5. あそこで本を<u>買っている</u>のはぼくの弟です。Ⓜ
   *Asoko de hon o <u>katte iru</u> no wa boku no otōto desu.*

✧ -てある [-*te aru*]

When ある [*aru*] "to exist (inanimate)" follows the -て [-*te*] form of a transitive verb, it indicates a resultative state. Compare the following:

(a) 戸が開いている。
   *To ga aite iru.*
   The door is open.

(b) 戸が開けてある。
   *To ga akete aru.*
   The door has been opened (by someone) (and is open now).

(c) 戸を開けてある。

*To o akete aru.*

(Someone, most likely the speaker) left the door open.

In all three examples, the outcome is the same: the opening of a door. However, the speaker's focus is different. In (a), the agent—that is, the person or thing that opened the door—is not important. What concerns the speaker here is the fact that the door is open. In (b), the agent may or may not be known to the speaker, but the speaker at least realizes that someone has opened it. In this construction, 〜が -てある [*~ga -te aru*], the subject is always inanimate. In (c) and similar sentences, the subject is usually known.

The 〜を -てある [*~o -te aru*] pattern is less common than 〜が -てある [*~ga -te aru*], probably because 〜を -ておく [*~o -te oku*] is used more often for the same situation. The pattern 〜を -てある [*~o -te aru*], like 〜を -ておく [*~o -te oku*], suggests that the subject of the verb has done something for a future purpose. Thus (d) and (e) have nearly the same meaning:

(d) 戸を開けてあります。

*To o akete arimasu.*

(e) 戸を開けておきました。

*To o akete okimashita.*

(I) opened the door (and have left it open for future convenience).

In (d) and (e), the speaker's message may be, "I'm keeping the door open, so you may come in whenever you want to."

In the next example, the -ている [*-te iru*] construction describes either that Mr. Sasaki possesses a certain past experience or his present state:

佐々木さんは日本に行っている。

*Sasaki-san wa Nihon ni itte iru.*

Mr. Sasaki has been to Japan.

*or* Mr. Sasaki went to Japan and is still there.

The following example with -てある [-*te aru*] means that the speaker does not have to go to the bank anymore because he or she has already gone.

わたしはもう銀行に行ってある。

*Watashi wa mō ginkō ni itte aru.*

I went to the bank already (so I don't have to go there anymore).

✧ -ておく [-*te oku*]

When used by itself, the verb おく [*oku*] means "to place" or "to put down." After the -て [-*te*] form, it indicates that the subject does something for a future purpose or convenience. The construction may also indicate a favor done for another person.

そこに置いておいて下さい。

*Soko ni oite oite kudasai.*

Please (place it and) leave it there (so that I can use it later).

花子さんに電話をかけておきます。

*Hanako-san ni denwa o kakete okimasu.*

I will call Hanako (so that she will know about the plan in advance).

---

● Negative Forms of -ておく [-te oku]

When negated, the -ておく [-te oku] construction takes on a different meaning depending on whether the -て [-te] form verb or おく [oku] is negated. Consider the following:

(a) 手紙は開けないでおきました。
   *Tegami wa akenai de okimashita.*
   I did not open the letter.

(b) 本を読んでおかなかったので……。
   *Hon o yonde okanakatta no de ...*
   I did not read the book (so I am unprepared).

In (a), the speaker has kept the letter without opening it, probably because she was asked not to open it or because she judged that it would be better to keep it sealed. In (b), the -ておかない [-te okanai] pattern merely indicates that the subject did not read the book in advance, although he had been told to do so.

---

✧ -てしまう [-te shimau]

The -てしまう [-te shimau] construction indicates that an action, motion, etc. is completed. This pattern often expresses the speaker's regret or disappointment, especially when the verb is intransitive.

> あの人は行ってしまった。　　　(intransitive verb)
> *Ano hito wa itte shimatta.*
> He has gone (and I'm sad).

> ジョーが全部食べてしまった。　(transitive verb)
> *Jō ga zenbu tabete shimatta.*

---

Joe ate it all.

*or* (I wanted to eat some, but) Joe ate it all.

In the second example, 食べてしまった [*tabete shimatta*] may simply mean that Joe ate it up, or it may also indicate the speaker's emotional reaction.

## ✧ -てみえる [*-te mieru*]

When みえる [*mieru*] "can be seen, appear" follows the -て [*-te*] form of verbs, it indicates the speaker's impression or assessment of the subject's condition. This pattern is appropriate only with descriptive verbs, such as ふとる [*futoru*] "to become fat," よごれる [*yogoreru*] "to become dirty," or つかれる [*tsukareru*] "to become tired." In other words, an expression such as たべてみえる [*tabete mieru*] is inappropriate since たべる [*taberu*] is not descriptive.

Some examples:

葉子さんは老けてみえます。

*Yōko-san wa fukete miemasu.*

Yōko looks old (i.e., older than her actual age).

疲れてみえる。

*Tsukarete mieru*

He looks tired.

## ✧ -てみる [*-te miru*]

When used after the -て [*-te*] form, みる [*miru*] "to see" takes on a meaning closer to "to try." In other words, the subject carries out an action to see the results. For example:

はじめてポイを食べてみました。

*Hajimete poi o tabete mimashita.*

I have eaten *poi* for the first time (to see how it tastes).

• Success and Failure

-てみた [-te mita] indicates that the subject actually
tried and achieved the result. When the speaker tried
or intended to do something but failed, ～うとした
[~ō to shita] is used.

そのケーキ、食べてみたけどわたしには甘すぎて（い
　　やだ／食べられない／おいしくない／etc.）。

*Sono kēki, tabete mita kedo watashi ni wa amasugite
(iya da / taberarenai / oishiku nai / etc.).*

I tasted the cake, but it was too sweet for me (so I
　　don't like it/I cannot eat it/it's not tasty/etc.).

早めに来ようと思ったのですが、客に来られて出られ
　　ませんでした。

*Hayame ni koyō to omotta no desu ga, kyaku ni kora-
rete deraremasen deshita.*

I had intended to come earlier, but a customer came
　　and so I couldn't leave.

一所懸命、納豆を食べようとしたのですが、やっぱり
　　だめでした。(lit., たべられませんでした)

*Isshō-kenmei, nattō o tabeyō to shita no desu ga, yap-
pari dame deshita.*

I tried my best to eat *natto*, but I just couldn't do it.

**❖ Review of Use of -て [-*te*] Forms**

Read the following passage and note how the -て [-*te*] forms
are used.

## 雪女 [*Yuki-onna*]

　昔、ある所に親子の猟師が<u>住んで</u>いました。父親の名前はもさく、息子の名前はみのきちでした。

　ある冬の日、もさくとみのきちは山に猟に出かけました。二人が獲物を<u>追って</u>、山の奥の方に<u>入って</u>行くと、急に暗く<u>なってきて</u>、大風が吹きだしました。あいにく雪も降り始めました。雪にとじこめられた二人は、山小屋に泊まることにしました。いろりの火で体が暖かく<u>なって</u>くると、すっかり眠く<u>なって</u>しまいました。もさくは、もう<u>眠ってしまって</u>いました。みのきちもうとうと<u>して</u>いました。

　みのきちがうとうと<u>して</u>いると、音も無く戸が明き、雪と一緒に美しい一人の娘が<u>入って</u>来ました。娘はまっすぐもさくの所に<u>歩いて</u>行くと、もさくの顔に白い息を吹きかけました。みのきちは恐ろしさで声も出ませんでした。しばらくすると、娘はみのきちの所に<u>やって来て</u>言いました。「お前はとても好い男だから命は取らないけれど、今夜のことは誰にも<u>言って</u>はいけないよ」と。みのきちは、言われたことを<u>守って</u>、誰にも言わないと約束しました。娘が<u>出て</u>行くのを見たみのきちは<u>急いで</u>もさくのところに<u>行って</u>みました。

　白い息をかけられたもさくはもうすっかり冷たく<u>なってしまって</u>いました。

　それから一年たちました。みのきちはあの夜のことは、誰にも言わないように<u>して</u>いました。

　ある寒い冬の夜、みのきちがいろりのそばで仕事を<u>して</u>いると、誰かが戸を叩く音がしました。「こんなおそく<u>なって</u>から人が来たことなんかないのに……誰だろう」と思いながら戸を<u>明けて</u>見ると、一人の美しい、色の白い娘が<u>立って</u>いました。娘は「道に<u>迷って</u>いるうちに、夜に<u>なって</u>しまいました。どうぞ今夜ここに<u>泊めて</u>下さい」と頼みました。かわいそうだと思ったみのきちは、

娘を泊めてやることにしました。

　また何年がたちました。みのきちをたずねて来た娘はみのきちの妻になっていました。妻はユキと言う名前でした。

　ある冬の夜のことでした。ユキはいろりのそばで針仕事をしていました。寝ころんでユキの美しい顔を見ていたみのきちは、「あれも、こんな夜だった」とつぶやきました。これを聞いたユキが「何があったんですか。話してください」と言いました。みのきちはうっかり約束を忘れて、全部話してしまいました。

　その時ユキが言いました。「お前は言われたことを忘れて、約束をやぶってしまった。子供のために、命はとらないけれど、私はもうここには居られない」と。

　ユキは、針仕事をやめると、静かに戸の外へ出て行きました。外はまた吹雪になりました。

*Mukashi, aru tokoro ni oyako no ryōshi ga sunde imashita. Chichioya no namae wa Mosaku, musuko no namae wa Minokichi deshita.*

*Aru fuyu no hi, Mosaku to Minokichi wa yama ni kari ni dekakemashita. Futari ga emono o otte, yama no oku no hō ni haitte iku to, kyū ni kuraku natte kite, ōkaze ga fukidashimashita. Ainiku yuki mo furihajimemashita. Yuki ni tojikomerareta futari wa, yamagoya ni tomaru koto ni shimashita. Irori no hi de karada ga atatakaku natte kuru to, sukkari nemuku natte shimaimashita. Mosaku wa, mō nemutte shimatte imashita. Minokichi mo utouto shite imashita.*

*Minokichi ga utouto shite iru to, oto mo naku to ga aki, yuki to issho ni utsukushii hitori no musume ga haitte kimashita. Musume wa massugu Mosaku no tokoro ni aruite iku to, Mosaku no kao ni shiroi iki o fukikakemashita. Minokichi wa osoroshisa de koe mo demasen deshita. Shibaraku suru to, musume wa Minokichi no tokoro ni yatte kite iimashita.*

*"Omae wa totemo ii otoko da kara inochi wa toranai keredo, kon'ya no koto wa dare ni mo <u>itte</u> wa ikenai yo" to. Minokichi wa, iwareta koto o <u>mamotte</u>, dare ni mo iwanai to yakusoku shimashita. Musume ga <u>dete</u> yuku no o mita Minokichi wa <u>isoide</u> Mosaku no tokoro ni <u>itte</u> mimashita.*

*Shiroi iki o kakerareta Mosaku wa mō sukkari tsumetaku <u>natte shimatte</u> imashita.*

*Sorekara ichinen tachimashita. Minokichi wa ano yoru no koto wa, dare ni mo iwanai yō ni <u>shite</u> imashita.*

*Aru samui fuyu no yoru, Minokichi ga irori no soba de shigoto o <u>shite</u> iru to, dare ka ga to o tataku oto ga shimashita. "Konna osoku <u>natte</u> kara hito ga kita koto nanka nai no ni … dare darō" to omoinagara to o <u>akete</u> miru to, hitori no utsukushii, iro no shiroi musume ga <u>tatte</u> imashita. Musume wa "Michi ni <u>mayotte</u> iru uchi ni, yoru ni <u>natte</u> shimaimashita. Dōzo kon'ya koko ni <u>tomete</u> kudasai" to tanomimashita. Kawaisō da to omotta Minokichi wa, musume o <u>tomete</u> yaru koto ni shimashita.*

*Mata nannen ga tachimashita. Minokichi o <u>tazunete</u> kita musume wa Minokichi no tsuma ni <u>natte</u> imashita. Tsuma wa Yuki to iu namae deshita.*

*Aru fuyu no yoru no koto deshita. Yuki wa irori no soba de hari-shigoto o <u>shite</u> imashita. <u>Nekoronde</u> Yuki no utsukushii kao o <u>mite</u> ita Minokichi wa, "Are mo, konna yoru datta" to tsubuyakimashita. Kore o kiita Yuki ga "Nani ga atta n' desu ka. <u>Hanashite</u> kudasai" to iimashita. Minokichi wa ukkari yakusoku o <u>wasurete</u>, zenbu <u>hanashite</u> shimaimashita.*

*Sono toki Yuki ga iimashita. "Omae wa iwareta koto o <u>wasurete</u>, yakusoku o <u>yabutte</u> shimatta. Kodomo no tame ni, inochi wa toranai keredo, watashi wa mō koko ni wa irarenai" to.*

*Yuki wa, hari-shigoto o yameru to, shizuka ni to no soto e <u>dete</u> ikimashita. Soto wa mata fubuki ni narimashita.*

| | |
|---|---|
| 昔 [*mukashi*] | olden days |
| ある所 [*aru tokoro*] | a certain place |
| 親子 [*oyako*] | parent(s) and child(ren) |
| 猟師 [*ryōshi*] | hunter |
| 猟 [*ryō*] | hunting |
| 獲物 [*emono*] | game, hunted animals |
| 追う [*ou*] | to chase after |
| 奥の方 [*oku no hō*] | inner part, depths |
| とじこめる [*tojikomeru*] | to confine |
| 山小屋 [*yamagoya*] | mountain shack |
| いろり [*irori*] | fireplace |
| うとうとする [*utouto suru*] | to doze off |
| 音も無く [*oto mo naku*] | without a sound |
| 娘 [*musume*] | maiden |
| 息 [*iki*] | breath |
| 吹きかける [*fukikakeru*] | to breathe on, to blow on |
| 恐ろしさで [*osoroshisa de*] | because of fear |
| 好い男 [*ii otoko*] | handsome man |
| 命を取る [*inochi o toru*] | to take life, to kill |
| 守る [*mamoru*] | to keep (a promise), to protect |
| 叩く [*tataku*] | to knock at, to beat, to hit |
| 音がする [*oto ga suru*] | there is a sound |
| 道に迷う [*michi ni mayou*] | to lose one's way |
| 妻 [*tsuma*] | wife |
| 針 [*hari*] | needle |
| 針仕事 [*hari-shigoto*] | needlework |
| 寝ころぶ [*nekorobu*] | to lie down |
| つぶやく [*tsubuyaku*] | to murmur |
| 吹雪 [*fubuki*] | blizzard, snowstorm |

# CONJUNCTIVE EXPRESSIONS: COMMON MISTAKES AND TROUBLESOME USAGES

## ■ Conjunctions

**•➔ SENTENCE** が [*ga*]／けど [*kedo*]（けれども [*keredomo*]、けれど [*keredo*]）

The conjunction が [*ga*] can usually be translated as "but," but not always. Here are some examples where が [*ga*] has a different meaning.

> 私は家庭の主婦ですが、子供が二人います。
>
> *Watashi wa katei no shufu desu ga, kodomo ga futari imasu.*
>
> I am a homemaker, and I have two children.

> 竜安寺は石の庭で有名だが、この石の庭は宇宙を表わしているという。
>
> *Ryōan-ji wa ishi no niwa de yūmei da ga, kono ishi no niwa wa uchū o arawashite iru to iu.*
>
> Ryōanji is famous for its rock garden. This rock garden is said to represent the universe.

> 一茶は「愛の人」と言われているが、全くこの名にふさわしい人であったようである。
>
> *Issa wa "ai no hito" to iwarete iru ga, mattaku kono na ni fusawashii hito de atta yō de aru.*
>
> Issa is called a "man of affection." It seems that he really was someone who deserved that name.

As you can see, が [ga] may also be translated as "and" or not at all. Thus が [ga] may simply join two separate or indirectly related statements.

Now compare the following variations of a sentence: (all Ⓜ)

(a) 僕も北海道に<u>行く</u><u>けど</u>稚内までは<u>行かない</u>よ。

*Boku mo Hokkaidō ni <u>iku kedo</u> Wakkanai made wa <u>ikanai</u> yo.*

(b) 僕も北海道に<u>行きます</u><u>が</u>／<u>けど</u>稚内までは<u>行きません</u>。

*Boku mo Hokkaidō ni <u>ikimasu ga/kedo</u> Wakkanai made wa <u>ikimasen</u>.*

(c) 僕も北海道に<u>行く</u><u>が</u>稚内までは<u>行かない</u>よ。

*Boku mo Hokkaidō ni <u>iku ga</u> Wakkanai made wa <u>ikanai</u> yo.*

(d) 僕も北海道に<u>行く</u><u>が</u>稚内までは<u>行きません</u>。

*Boku mo Hokkaidō ni <u>iku ga</u> Wakkanai made wa <u>ikimasen</u>.*

(e) 僕も北海道に<u>行きます</u><u>が</u>稚内までは<u>行かない</u>。

*Boku mo Hokkaidō ni <u>ikimasu ga</u> Wakkanai made wa <u>ikanai</u>.*

(f) 僕も北海道に<u>行く</u><u>けど</u>稚内までは<u>行きません</u>。

*Boku mo Hokkaidō ni <u>iku kedo</u> Wakkanai made wa <u>ikimasen</u>.*

I'll also go to Hokkaidō, but I won't go as far as Wakkanai.

Versions (a) and (b) are the most appropriate and natural sounding. Version (c) is grammatically correct, but the use of が [ga] with the informal form of a verb, adjective, or the copula だ [da] may sound stiff or awkward. The use of が [ga] after an informal ending is most common in the speech of older men, as in the next example:

> わたしも/わしも昔はよくゴルフをやったものだが、今はもう……。
>
> *Watashi mo / Washi mo mukashi wa yoku gorufu o yatta mono da ga, ima wa mō ...*
>
> I also used to golf a lot, but not anymore.

Versions (d) and (e) above are very awkward due to the mixing of the formal and informal forms. Version (f) is similar to (d), but it is acceptable, probably because けど [*kedo*] makes the expression softer and less formal.

To summarize, INFORMAL けど [*kedo*] + INFORMAL and FORMAL けど／が [*kedo/ga*] + FORMAL are the most appropriate combinations. The conjunctions けれども [*keredomo*] and けれど [*keredo*] are less colloquial than けど [*kedo*]; けれど [*keredo*] and けど [*kedo*] are more common in conversation than in writing.

---

- Summary of が [*ga*]

**NOUN** が [*ga*]

◇ *After Interrogatives and to Point Out a Specific Object*

A: 何がありますか。
B: 本があります。
*A: Nani ga arimasu ka.*
*B: Hon ga arimasu.*
A: What do you have?
B: We have books.

A: どれがマンゴーですか。
B: これです。
*A: Dore ga mangō desu ka.*
*B: Kore desu.*
A: Which is the mango?
B: This one.

A:  何がいいですか。
B:  それがいいです。
*A:  Nani ga ii desu ka.*

---

*B:*    *Sore ga ii desu.*
A:    Which would you like?
B:    That one.

◇ *To Introduce a New and Unfamiliar Subject*

昔、おじいさんとおばあさんが住んでいました。
*Mukashi, ojiisan to obaasan ga sunde imashita.*
Once upon a time there lived an old man and an old
   woman.

田中という方がいらっしゃいました。
*Tanaka to iu kata ga irasshaimashita.*
A person named Tanaka has arrived.

◇ *Subject of Noun Modifier:* NOUN が [*ga*] VERB/ AD-
JECTIVE/ADJECTIVAL NOUN + NOUN

氷河期が来ると言う説がある。
*Hyōga-ki ga kuru to iu setsu ga aru.*
There's a theory that an ice age is coming.

コーヒーがおいしい店
*kōhī ga oishii mise*
a shop with good coffee

おかしが好きな子供
*okashi ga suki na kodomo*
children who like sweets

SENTENCE A が [*ga*]、 SENTENCE B

◇ *"But"*

たしかにこれはいいですが、わたしにはちょっと高す
   ぎます。

---

*Tashika ni kore wa ii desu ga, watashi ni wa chotto takasugimasu.*

It's true that this is nice, but it's a bit too expensive for me.

行くことは行ったんですが、会えなかったんです。

*Iku koto wa itta n' desu ga, aenakatta n' desu.*

I did go, but I wasn't able to meet her.

❖ *"And" or Not Translated*

明日から休みなのですが、三連休なので伊豆の温泉に行こうかと思っているところです。

*Asu kara yasumi na no desu ga, san-renkyū na no de Izu no onsen ni ikō ka to omotte iru tokoro desu.*

We have a vacation from tomorrow, and it is a three-day vacation, so I am wondering if I should go to a hot spring in Izu.

私もあの人は知っていますが、とてもいい人ですよ。

*Watashi mo ano hito wa shitte imasu ga, totemo ii hito desu yo.*

I know her, too. She's really nice.

ケンは大学に行っていますが、英語の勉強がしたいようです。

*Ken wa daigaku ni itte imasu ga, eigo no benkyō ga shitai yō desu.*

Ken's going to college. He seems to want to study English.

あしたの面接のことですが、何時からでしょうか。

*Ashita no mensetsu no koto desu ga, nanji kara deshō ka.*

Regarding tomorrow's interview—when does it start?

❖ *Deletion of* SENTENCE B *to Soften a Statement*

行けると思いますが……（まだはっきりは分かりません）。

*Ikeru to omoimasu ga ... (mada hakkiri wa wakarima-sen.*

I think I can go (but I don't know for sure yet).

わたしもこれが欲しいんですが……（ありますか）。

*Watashi mo kore ga hoshii n' desu ga ... (arimasu ka).*

I would also like this one (do you have it?).

山口さんもあした来ると言ったと思うんですが……（ちがいますか）。

*Yamaguchi-san mo ashita kuru to itta to omou n' desu ga ... (chigaimasu ka).*

I think Ms. Yamaguchi said that she would come to-morrow, too (am I wrong?).

❖ のに [*no ni*]

The conjunction のに [*no ni*] expresses the speaker's attitude, such as surprise, envy, admiration, or resentment. This contrasts with けど [*kedo*] and が [*ga*], which just connect two sentences. In the following examples, the のに [*no ni*] in (b) and (d) shows the speaker's feeling, in contrast to the more objective けど [*kedo*] in (a) and (c):

(a) ずいぶん雨が降ってる<u>けど</u>、やっぱり行くの？

*Zuibun ame ga futte 'ru kedo, yappari iku no?*

It's raining hard. Are you still going (as you planned)?

(b) こんなに雨が降ってる<u>のに</u>、（それでも）やっぱり行くの？

*Konna ni ame ga futte 'ru no ni, (sore de mo) yappari iku no?*

It's raining this hard, and you're still going?! (I can't believe it. / I don't think you should go.)

(c) 彼は若い<u>けど</u>、もう部長になってるようよ。Ⓕ
*Kare wa wakai kedo, mō buchō ni natte 'ru yō yo.*
He is young, but he is already a department head.

(d) 彼は若い<u>のに</u>、もう部長なんですって！(すごいわね) Ⓕ
*Kare wa wakai no ni, mō buchō nan desu tte! (sugoi wa
ne)*
Even though he is still young, I heard that he is already a
department head. (Isn't that amazing?!)

In the next example, the two halves of the sentence are
not directly related. Here, the のに [*no ni*] indicates that the
second half of the sentence is the speaker's reaction to the
first half.

まだ子供な<u>のに</u>かわいそうだ。
*Mada kodomo na no ni kawaisō da.*

The above sentence may express the speaker's anger at a
news report about young boys carrying guns and fighting
shoulder to shoulder with adult soldiers. What the speaker
wants to say is: "I feel sorry for the boys. After all, they are
still young! (and yet they are made to fight with adult soldiers like that!)" The version まだ子供だ<u>けど</u>かわいそうだ
[*Mada kodomo da kedo kawaisō da.*] would be incorrect, because けど [*kedo*] cannot conjoin unrelated sentences.

In conversation, のに [*no ni*] may be used at the end of a
sentence to show the speaker's frustration or resentment.

(a) A: おいしいって言ってたからきのうあのレストラン
に行ったけど休みだったわよ。Ⓕ
B: だから、月曜日は閉ってるって言った<u>のに</u>……。

73

A: *Oishii tte itte 'ta kara kinō ano resutoran ni itta kedo yasumi datta wa yo.*

B: *Dakara, Getsuyō-bi wa shimatte 'ru tte itta <u>no ni</u> ...*

A: You said that restaurant was good, so I went there yesterday, but it was closed.

B: That's why I told you that the restaurant is closed on Mondays! (Why didn't you listen to me?! Yesterday was Monday!)

(b) C: ちっとも食べてないじゃない？人がせっかく作っ<br>た<u>のに</u>……。

D: ごめん。おいしいけどもうおなかがいっぱいなん<br>だよ。Ⓜ

C: *Chittomo tabete nai ja nai? Hito ga sekkaku tsukutta <u>no ni</u> ...*

D: *Gomen. Oishii kedo mō onaka ga ippai nan da yo.*

C: You've eaten almost nothing. (Why?) I made a special effort to make it ...

D: I'm sorry. It's delicious, but I'm already full.

---

- だ [*da*] and な [*na*]

The copula だ [*da*] becomes な [*na*] before のに [*no ni*]. Before けど [*kedo*], though, だ [*da*] remains だ.

| 女の人<u>だ</u> | ⇨ | 女の人<u>な</u><u>のに</u> |
|---|---|---|
| *onna no hito <u>da</u>* | | *onna no hito <u>na no ni</u>* |
| | | 女の人<u>だけど</u> |
| | | *onna no hito <u>da kedo</u>* |
| きれい<u>だ</u> | ⇨ | きれい<u>な</u><u>のに</u> |
| *kirei <u>da</u>* | | *kirei <u>na no ni</u>* |
| | | きれい<u>だけど</u> |
| | | *kirei <u>da kedo</u>* |

---

*Exercise 6* ────────────────────────

Fill in the blanks with either の に [*no ni*] or け ど [*kedo*]. Insert the copula だ [*da*] or な [*na*] where appropriate.

1. 大した仕事でもない＿＿、大げさに騒ぎたてている。
   *Taishita shigoto de mo nai ___, ōgesa ni sawagi-tatete iru.*

2. 忙しい＿＿、文句ばかり言って、ちっとも働かない。
   *Isogashii ___, monku bakari itte, chittomo hata-rakanai.*

3. 雨が止んだ＿＿、そろそろ出かけない？
   *Ame ga yanda ___, sorosoro dekakenai?*

4. 和田さんはいい人＿＿、どうして皆に嫌われるのかな？
   *Wada-san wa ii hito ___, dōshite minna ni kira-wareru no ka na?*

5. 体は小さい＿＿、力は強いんだよ。
   *Karada wa chiisai ___, chikara wa tsuyoi n' da yo.*

6. あの人はいい人＿＿、結婚はしたくない。
   *Ano hito wa ii hito ___, kekkon wa shitaku nai.*

7. 天気がいい＿＿、家でゴロゴロしないで、散歩にでも行ったらどう？
   *Tenki ga ii ___, ie de gorogoro shinai de, sanpo ni de mo ittara dō?*

8. あの子はおなかがすいている＿＿、やせがまんしている。
   *Ano ko wa onaka ga suite iru ___, yase-gaman shite iru.*

9. おなかはすいていた＿＿＿、食べる暇がなくて今日
は昼ご飯をぬいてしまった。

*Onaka wa suite ita ___, taberu hima ga nakute kyō
wa hiru-gohan o nuite shimatta.*

10. 雨は降っている＿＿＿、傘をさすほどではない。

*Ame wa futte iru ___, kasa o sasu hodo de wa nai.*

## ■ Reason and Cause

**•◆ Sentence A。だから [*dakara*] Sentence B。**

When the conjunctive だから [*dakara*] joins sentences A and
B, sentence A expresses a reason or cause, while the sentence
B expresses the result or effect. It can often be translated as
"so," "therefore," or "that's why."

このアパートは"ペットお断り"なんですって。だか
ら犬は飼えないのよ。Ⓕ

*Kono apāto wa "petto okotowari" nan desu tte. Dakara
inu wa kaenai no yo.*

We've been told that pets are not allowed in this apartment. That's why we can't have a dog.

急に用ができてしまってね。だから今日は一緒に行け
ないけど、今度またね。

*Kyū ni yō ga dekite shimatte ne. Dakara kyō wa issho ni
ikenai kedo, kondo mata ne.*

Some urgent business has come up, so I can't go with you
today. Next time, I'll go.

だから [*dakara*] is more commonly used in casual or informal situations. Its use in sentences like the following may
sound rough, impolite, or awkward.

(a) 今日、面接があるという電話連絡をいただきました。
だから参りましたのですけれど……。

*Kyō, mensetsu ga aru to iu denwa-renraku o itadakimashita. Dakara mairimashita no desu keredo ...*

I received a message saying that there would be an interview today, so I came ...

(b) だから、今ここで倫理学とは何かなどと、決定的な定義をくだすことは不可能である。Ⓜ

*Dakara, ima koko de rinri-gaku to wa nani ka nado to, kettei-teki na teigi o kudasu koto wa fukanō de aru.*

Therefore, it is impossible (for me) to provide a decisive definition of "ethics" right here and now.

The situation in (a) is formal and the speaker is trying to speak politely. それで [*sore de*] would more appropriate than だから [*dakara*]. Sentence (b) is not conversational and the topic is not casual, so したがって [*shitagatte*] is more appropriate.

In the following examples, だから [*dakara*] shows the speaker's frustration, offended attitude, or disgust.

だから、何だって言うんですか？
*Dakara, nan datte iu n' desu ka?*
So, what?! (What are you grumbling about?)

A: この間行ったばかりなのに、また行くの？
B: だから、行くのやめたって言ったでしょう！
*A: Kono aida itta bakari na no ni, mata iku no?*
*B: Dakara, iku no yameta tte itta deshō?*
A: Are you going again? You've just been there!
B: I decided not to go. I told you that, didn't I?

What B really wants to say may be, "Don't keep asking me the same question! You're driving me crazy."

**•◦ SENTENCE A** から／ので [*kara / no de*] **SENTENCE B**

The conjuctives から [*kara*] and ので [*no de*] are translated as "because," where sentence A is a reason or cause for sentence B. In Japanese, the sentence describing a reason or cause always precedes the sentence giving the result or effect. For example:

高すぎた<u>から</u>／<u>ので</u>、買わなかった。

*Takasugita <u>kara</u> / <u>no de</u>, kawanakatta.*
  *reason*              *result*

I didn't buy it <u>because</u> it was too expensive.
  *result*                    *reason*

から [*kara*] and ので [*node*] are used similarly, but they are not always interchangeable. For example, ので [*no de*] sounds softer than から [*kara*] . The origin of ので [*no de*] is the -て [*-te*] form of のだ [*no da*], and so it functions like the -て [*-te*] form. As mentioned in the -て [*-te*] section, the basic function of -て [*-te*] is to conjoin two sentences. The first sentence may also show a reason or cause for the second, but not directly or explicitly. Sometimes indirectness and vagueness are considered less aggressive and therefore desirable.

ので [*no de*] is more appropriate than から [*kara*] in formal sentences and polite speech. Consider the following example:

家から送って来ました<u>から</u>、どうぞ。

*Ie kara okutte kimashita <u>kara</u>, dōzo.*
These were sent here by my family. Please have some.

The speaker is offering a guest some fruit or other food that has been sent from the speaker's family. Here, から [*kara*] sounds rough or impolite. A better version would be

家から送って来ました<u>ので</u>、どうぞ [Ie kara okutte ki-mashita <u>no de</u>, dōzo].

In the A ので [no de]、 B pattern, the sentences A and B are connected sequentially or concurrently, and their topic is the same or related. This is similar to the A -て [-te] B pattern. In the following examples, either pattern is acceptable:

列車が<u>おくれて</u>、二時間待たされた。
*Ressha ga <u>okurete</u>, niji-kan matasareta.*
列車が<u>おくれたので</u>、二時間待たされた。
*Ressha ga <u>okureta no de</u>, niji-kan matasareta.*
The train was delayed, so we had to wait for two hours.

In the sentence above, から [kara] would sound awkward or childish. It might even suggest that the speaker is implying that the delay was the train's fault. In the next sentence, for example, the speaker blames his delay on the bus:

すみません。バスが遅く来たから遅れました。
*Sumimasen. Basu ga osoku kita kara okuremashita.*
Sorry. I'm late because the bus was late.

Despite these rules, sometimes the choice between から [kara] and ので [no de] is only a matter of personal preference or regional variation.

---

• Restrictions on から [kara]

から [kara] clearly spells out a reason or cause, so it is not appropriate to use から [kara] (especially with ん です [n' desu]) to express a desire or request or to ask for permission. Such sentences may sound arrogant and self-centered. For example, the next statement is very awkward:

わたしも行きたいんです<u>から</u>、一緒に行ってもいいですか。

*Watashi mo ikitai n' desu <u>kara</u>, issho ni itte mo ii desu ka.*

I want to go, too, so can I go with you?

けれど [*keredo*], けど [*kedo*], or が [*ga*] would be more appropriate here:

わたしも行きたいんです<u>けれど</u>、一緒に行ってもいいですか。

*Watashi mo ikitai n' desu <u>keredo</u>, issho ni itte mo ii desu ka.*

わたしも行きたいんだ<u>けど</u>、一緒に行ってもいい？

*Watashi mo ikitai n' da <u>kedo</u>, issho ni itte mo ii?*

わたしも行きたいんです<u>が</u>、一緒に行ってもいいでしょうか。

*Watashi mo ikitai n' desu <u>ga</u>, issho ni itte mo ii deshō ka.*

When two sentences are linked by ので [*no de*], the reason or cause provided in the first sentence should be well-grounded and factual, and objectively accepted by others. The reason provided by から [*kara*], on the other hand, may be invalid or unconvincing, such as an opinion or conjecture of the speaker's. For example:

今年は台風が多そうだから、非常食を買っておいた方がいいだろう。Ⓜ

*Kotoshi wa taifū ga ōsō da kara, hijō-shoku o katte oita hō ga ii darō.*

There seem likely to be a lot of typhoons this year, so I think we should stock up on emergency rations.

## ➡ 〜おかげで ／ 〜せい [*~okage de/~sei*]

Both of these expressions mean "because of," but 〜おかげ
で [*~okage de*] is usually used when the speaker is trying to
show appreciation, while 〜 せい [*~sei*] is used when the
speaker is trying to place blame on something or someone.

救助隊の皆様の<u>おかげで</u>助かりました。ありがとうご
ざいました。

*Kyūjo-tai no minasama no <u>okage de</u> tasukarimashita. Ari-
gatō gozaimashita.*

I was saved because of the efforts of the rescue team.
Thank you very much.

コンサート、始まっちゃたよ。君が三十分もおくれて
来た<u>せ</u>いだぞ。Ⓜ

*Konsāto, hajimatchatta yo. Kimi ga sanjuppun mo okurete
kita <u>sei</u> da zo.*

The concert has started already. It's your fault (that we
missed the beginning) because you came thirty minutes
late.

Sometimes, though, おかげで [*okage de*] can also be
used to place blame:

ピックニックの最中に大雨に降られて……。<u>おかげで</u>
風邪、ひいちゃったわ。Ⓕ

*Pikunikku no saichū ni ōame ni furarete ... <u>Okage de</u>
kaze, hiichatta wa.*

Because of the heavy rain during our picnic, I ended up
catching a cold.

As shown by the above example, おかげで [*okage de*]
can be unmodified. However, せいで [*sei de*] must have a
modifier:

熱のせいで　　　　　*netsu no sei de*
　　　　　　　　　　because of a fever
年をとったせいで　　*toshi o totta sei de*
　　　　　　　　　　because of growing old
高かったせいか　　　*takakatta sei ka*
　　　　　　　　　　probably because it was too expensive

---

● もの [*mono*]

The sentence particle もの [*mono*] also expresses a reason or an excuse. It is often used by women when trying to evade responsibility.

仕方がないでしょ。バスがなかなか来なかったんだもの。Ⓕ
*Shikata ga nai desho. Basu ga nakanaka konakatta n' da mono.*
I can't help it. The bus didn't come for a long time (and that's why I'm late).

ごめんなさい。急に客が来たもので、出られなかったの。Ⓕ
*Gomennasai. Kyū ni kyaku ga kita mono de, derarena-katta no.*
I'm sorry. I had an unexpected guest, so I couldn't leave (on time).

---

## ■ Partial Negation

●◆ SENTENCE （だ）からといって [*(da) kara to itte*]、SENTENCE **B**

（だ）からといって [*(da) kara to itte*] is a set phrase meaning roughly "while it may be true that" or "just because." It is often used with negative endings such as とは限らない、（という）わけにはいかない [*to wa kagiranai, (to iu) wake*

---

*ni wa ikanai*], or ということ／わけではない [*to iu koto /
wake de wa nai*].

雨の日が続いた<u>からといって</u>、これで水不足の問題が
解消したわけではない。

*Ame no hi ga tsuzuita <u>kara to itte</u>, kore de mizu-busoku
no mondai ga kaishō shita wake de wa nai.*

Simply because it rained several days in a row doesn't
mean that the water-shortage problem has been solved.

金持ち<u>だからといって</u>幸福だとは限らないっていうの
は本当らしい。

*Kanemochi <u>da kara to itte</u> kōfuku da to wa kagiranai tte
iu no wa hontō rashii.*

It seems to be true that being rich doesn't necessarily
mean that you're happy.

休み<u>だからといって</u>遊んでばかりいるわけにはいかない。

*Yasumi <u>da kara to itte</u> asonde bakari iru wake ni wa ikanai.*

Just because I'm on vacation doesn't mean that I can
spend all my time playing around.

（だ）からといって [*(da) kara to itte*] may also be used
without a preceding clause to mean "nevertheless" or "not
necessarily":

わたしもあの人は嫌いよ。でもね<u>だからといって</u>、招
待状をもらったら行かないわけにいかないでしょ。Ⓕ

*Watashi mo ano hito wa kirai yo. Demo ne <u>da kara to
itte</u>, shōtai-jō o morattara ikanai wake ni ikanai desho.*

I don't like him/her, either. But, still, if we get an invita-
tion, we'll have no choice but to go, right?

たしかにあの人は荒っぽいけど、<u>だからといって</u>悪い
人だとは限らないと思う。

*Tashika ni ano hito wa arappoi kedo, <u>da kara to itte</u>
warui hito da to wa kagiranai to omou.*

He/she certainly is rough, but I don't think that necessarily makes him/her a bad person.

⏺ たしかに [*tashika ni*] SENTENCE A が／けど [*ga / kedo*]、
SENTENCE B.

たしかに [*tashika ni*] SENTENCE A. でも／しかし [*demo /
shikashi*]、SENTENCE B.

These patterns indicate that the speaker agrees with statement A but does not accept the conclusions drawn from it. Statement B expresses these reservations.

これは<u>たしかに</u>ものがいい<u>けど</u>、ちょっと値がはりす
ぎるんじゃない？

*Kore wa <u>tashika ni</u> mono ga ii <u>kedo</u>, chotto ne ga hari-
sugiru n' ja nai?*

This certainly is of good quality, but don't you think it costs too much?

<u>たしかに</u>そう言いましたよ。<u>でも</u>そんな意味で言った
んじゃありません。

*<u>Tashika ni</u> sō iimashita yo. <u>Demo</u> sonna imi de itta n' ja
arimasen.*

Certainly that's what I said, but I didn't mean it in that way.

⏺ SENTENCE A. ただ／ただし [*tada / tadashi*] SENTENCE B.

This pattern indicates that B is a condition or requirement for A.

やってあげますよ。<u>ただ</u>、あしたまでは忙しいから、
その後になりますけど……。

*Yatte agemasu yo. <u>Tada</u>, ashita made wa isogashii kara,
sono ato ni narimasu kedo ...*

I'll do it for you, but I'll be busy until tomorrow, so it will have to be after that.

貸し出しは出来ます。ただし、月曜日の朝までには返却して下さい。

*Kashidashi wa dekimasu. <u>Tadashi</u>, Getsuyōbi no asa made ni wa henkyaku shite kudasai.*

We can lend you the book. However, please return it by Monday morning.

## ●❖ SENTENCE A といっても／としても [*to itte mo / toshite mo*]、SENTENCE B

In these patterns, B partially negates A. With といっても [*to itte mo*], the information in A is factual but very general, so the speaker provides more specific information in B. In the としても [*toshite mo*] pattern, sentence A indicates an assumption about some possible event or situation.

むし暑い<u>といっても</u>、東京の夏と比べれば、ずっと涼しいですけどね。

*Mushi atsui <u>to itte mo</u>, Tōkyō no natsu to kurabereba, zutto suzushii desu kedo ne.*

Even though it is hot and humid here, compared to the summer in Tokyo, it's much cooler …

おすしが大好きだ<u>といっても</u>、そんなには食べられないわよ。Ⓕ

*Osushi ga daisuki da <u>to itte mo</u>, sonna ni wa taberarenai wa yo.*

I do like sushi a lot, but even so I can't eat that much.

いつか日本に行ける<u>としても</u>、まだ二、三年先のことだと思う。

*Itsuka Nihon ni ikeru <u>toshite mo</u>, mada ni, san-nen saki no koto da to omou.*

Even if I am able to go to Japan someday, I imagine it will be two or three years from now.

台風が来た<u>としても</u>、この建物は大丈夫だろう。Ⓜ

*Taifū ga kita <u>toshite mo</u>, kono tatemono wa daijōbu darō.*

Even if a typhoon were to come, this building should be safe.

**•◦ としたら／とすれば／とすると [*to shitara / to sureba / to suru to*] vs. としても [*toshite mo*]**

The connectives としたら／とすれば／とすると [*to shitara / to sureba / to suru to*] are often confused with としても [*toshite mo*], probably because both can be translated as "if." However, there are distinctions that must be kept in mind.

---

• とする [*to suru*]

とする [*to suru*] is used for making an assumption.

ＡとＢの長さは等しいものとする。

*A to B no nagasa wa hitoshii mono to suru.*

We assume that the lengths of A and B are the same.

---

In the pattern SENTENCE A とすれば／としたら／とすると [*to sureba / to shitara / to suru to*], SENTENCE B, statement B describes how the statement A will be fulfilled, satisfied, or realized. In SENTENCE A としても [*toshite mo*] SENTENCE B, statement B does not satisfy the assumptions of statement A. In other words, B does not fully fulfill or support the assumption or conditions stated by A. In the としても [*toshite mo*] pattern, statement B may also suggest the speaker's reluctance or unwillingness.

---

日本に行く<u>としたら</u>、二、三週間はいたいですね。

*Nihon ni iku <u>to shitara</u>, ni, san-shūkan wa itai desu ne.*

Assuming that I go to Japan (If I go to Japan), I want to stay for at least two or three weeks.

あしたのパーティー？　行く<u>としても</u>長くいる気はないわ。Ⓕ

*Ashita no pātī? Iku <u>toshite mo</u> nagaku iru ki wa nai wa.*

Tomorrow's party? Even if I go I have no intention of staying long.

## ■ Idiomatic Expressions

The following are some examples of idiomatic expressions similar to the patterns in the preceding sections.

そろそろ仲直りにした方がいいと思うんだけど、彼の方はまだ怒っているらしい。<u>そうかといって</u>、こちらから謝まるのはしゃくだし……。

*Sorosoro naka-naori ni shita hō ga ii to omou n' da kedo, kare no hō wa mada okotte iru rashii. <u>Sōka to itte</u>, kochira kara ayamaru no wa shaku da shi …*

I think it's about time for us to make up, but he still seems to be angry at me. <u>But still</u>, I hate to apologize first …

やっとドルが高くなった。<u>そうかといって</u>、この状態が続くとも思えない。

*Yatto doru ga takaku natta. <u>Sōka to itte</u>, kono jōtai ga tsuzuku to mo omoenai.*

Finally, the dollar went up, <u>but still</u> I don't expect this situation to last.

<u>なんにしても</u>、大事故にならずに済んでよかったですねえ。

*<u>Nan ni shite mo</u>, dai-jiko ni narazu ni sunde yokatta desu nee.*

<u>In any event</u>, I am glad you didn't get involved in a serious accident.

A: 一緒に行くんでしょう？

B: 多分。とにかく<u>行くにしても行かないにしても</u>電話する。

*A: Issho ni iku n' deshō?*

*B: Tabun. Tonikaku <u>iku ni shite mo ikanai ni shite mo</u> denwa suru.*

A: You're going with us, aren't you?

B: Probably. Anyway, <u>whether I go or not</u>, I'll call you.

A: あの人、話しかけて来たけど。知ってるの？

B: 時々バスで一緒になるのよね。<u>それにしても</u>、どうしてわたしの名前、知ってたのかしら。Ⓕ

*A: Ano hito, hanashi kakete kita kedo. Shitte 'ru no?*

*B: Tokidoki basu de issho ni naru no yo ne. <u>Sore ni shite mo</u>, dōshite watashi no namae, shitte 'ta no kashira.*

A: Do you know the guy who came over to speak with you?

B: Sometimes we're on the same bus. <u>Even so</u>, I wonder how he knew my name.

それにしても [*sore ni shite mo*] is often used merely to introduce the next statement in the same manner as だけど [*da kedo*] or でも [*demo*]. It may emphasize the importance of the statement that follows, but it does not add any meaning. For example:

<u>それにしても</u>不思議だねえ、三十年後にまた同じところでバッタリ出会うなんて。Ⓜ

*<u>Sore ni shite mo</u> fushigi da nee, sanjūnen-go ni mata onaji tokoro de battari deau nante.*

It's *really* incredible! Imagine running into you in the same spot after thirty years!

• ところで [*tokoro de*]

ところで [*tokoro de*] after the -た [*-ta*] form may replace としても [*toshite mo*]. In the ところで [*tokoro de*] pattern, though, the ところで [*tokoro de*] indicates the speaker's sense of resignation or hopelessness.

行った<u>ところで</u>、どうせ会えるわけじゃないのだから
......。

*Itta <u>tokoro de</u>, dōse aeru wake ja nai no da kara ...*

Even if I go, there's little chance that I'll be able to meet them anyway.

あの人に何を言った<u>ところで</u>何の役にもたたない。

*Ano hito ni nani o itta <u>tokoro de</u> nan no yaku ni mo tatanai.*

No matter what you tell her, it's no use.

## ■ Purpose and Reason: SENTENCE のに [no ni]/ SENTENCE ために [tame ni]

Both のに [*no ni*] and ために [*tame ni*] are used with the dictionary forms of verbs and can be translated as "in order to." Keep in mind, though, that のに [*no ni*] refers to the process of fulfilling the purpose rather than the purpose itself.

In the first example below, the speaker is saying that the process of getting on the train is hard. That is why のに [*no ni*] is used.

ラッシュ・アワーには電車に乗る<u>のに</u>大変だ。

*Rasshu-awā ni wa densha ni noru <u>no ni</u> taihen da.*

It is hard to get on the train during rush hour.

In the next example, the speaker uses ために [*tame ni*] to

indicate the purpose of getting up at four o'clock (that is, to catch the six o'clock bus). Here, what is hard is getting up at four o'clock, not catching the bus.

六時のバスに乗る<u>ためには</u>四時までにはおきなければ
間に合わないから大変なのよ。Ⓕ

*Rokuji no basu ni noru <u>tame ni</u> wa yoji made ni wa oki-nakereba maniawanai kara taihen na no yo.*

It's hard, because if I don't get up by four o'clock, I will miss the six o'clock bus.

Because のに [*no ni*] refers to the process of doing something, it is safer to use ために [*tame ni*] to indicate a reason or purpose. A sentence like 本を買うのに本屋に行く [*hon o kau no ni honya ni iku*] is awkward, because のに [*no ni*] seems to indicate the purpose of going to a bookstore, not the process of buying a book. Here, ために [*tame ni*] would be better. However, if the following sentence indicates necessity, obligation, requirement, advice, or suggestion, then のに [*no ni*] is natural and not awkward.

Some examples:

(a) これを買う<u>のに</u>は浅草まで行かなければならない。
*Kore o kau <u>no ni</u> wa Asakusa made ikanakereba naranai.*
We have to go as far as Asakusa to buy this.

(b) この大学を卒業する<u>のに</u>何単位要るの？
*Kono daigaku o sotsugyō suru <u>no ni</u> nan-tan'i iru no?*
How many credits do you need to graduate from this college?

(c) 卒業する<u>ために</u>はあと何単位要るの？
*Sotsugyō suru <u>tame ni</u> wa ato nan-tan'i iru no?*
How many more credits do you need in order to graduate?

The focus of sentence (b) is the process of completing the graduation requirements, so のに [*no ni*] is used. In (c), the focus is on the goal of graduating, so ために [*tame ni*] is used.

---

### Exercise 7 ———————————————

Fill in the blanks with either のに or ために.

1. フライド・チキンを食べる＿＿は手を使う方が楽だ。Ⓜ
   *Furaido-chikin o taberu ___ wa te o tsukau hō ga raku da.*

2. このケーキを作る＿＿どのぐらい時間がかかりましたか。
   *Kono kēki o tsukuru ___ dono gurai jikan ga kakari-mashita ka.*

3. 今晩スキヤキを作る＿＿マーケットで肉を買って来た。
   *Konban sukiyaki o tsukuru ___ māketto de niku o katte kita.*

4. 友だちに会う＿＿わざわざ渋谷駅まで行ったのに、彼女はとうとう来なかった。
   *Tomodachi ni au ___ wazawaza Shibuya-eki made itta no ni, kanojo wa tōtō konakatta.*

5. この町がすっかり復興する＿＿は、まだまだ時間がかかりそうだ。Ⓜ
   *Kono machi ga sukkari fukkō suru ___ wa, mada-mada jikan ga kakarisō da.*

6. 熱帯雨林を救う＿＿寄付をお願いします。
   *Nettai-urin o sukuu ___ kifu o onegai shimasu.*

7. すみません。東京ドームに行く＿＿は、どう行けばいいのでしょうか。

---

*Sumimasen. Tōkyō-dōmu ni iku* ___ *wa, dō ikeba ii no deshō ka.*

8. カキの木が実をつけるようになる____は８年かかるそうです。

   *Kaki no ki ga mi o tsukeru yō ni naru* ___ *wa hachi-nen kakaru sō desu.*

9. 東京から大阪まで行く____新幹線だといくらぐらいかかるのかしら。Ⓕ

   *Tōkyō kara Ōsaka made iku* ___ *Shinkan-sen da to ikura gurai kakaru no kashira.*

10. あすの試験にパスする____、今夜は徹夜で勉強します。

    *Asu no shiken ni pasu suru* ___, *kon'ya wa tetsuya de benkyō shimasu.*

11. 都心を離れればもっと安く家が手に入るからと思ったんだけど、始発の電車に乗る____毎朝早く起きなければならないのでつらいよ。Ⓜ

    *Toshin o hanarereba motto yasuku ie ga te ni hairu kara to omotta n' da kedo, shihatsu no densha ni noru* ___ *maiasa hayaku okinakereba naranai no de tsurai yo.*

12. いつも銀座まで地下鉄で行くんだけど、ラッシュの時は大変だよ。乗る____押されたり突きとばされたりして。Ⓜ

    *Itsumo Ginza made chikatetsu de iku n' da kedo, rasshu no toki wa taihen da yo.*

# ■Hearsay: によると [ni yoru to]

The connecting phrase によると [*ni yoru to*] indicates a source of information. For example:

ラジオによると、京都は今桜が満開です。

*Rajio ni yoru to, Kyōto wa ima sakura ga mankai desu.*

According to the radio, the cherry blossoms are now in
   full bloom in Kyoto.

Do not confuse によると [*ni yoru to*] with によって [*ni
yotte*], which means "by means of" or "depending on." The
next two sentences are incorrect because によって [*ni yotte*]
is being used to indicate a source of information:

天気予報によって、あしたは午後から大雨になるよう
　です。

*Tenki-yohō ni yotte, ashita wa gogo kara ōame ni naru yō
   desu.*

手紙によって、彼は来月結婚します。

*Tegami ni yotte, kare wa raigetsu kekkon shimasu.*

Replacing the によって [*ni yotte*] with によると [*ni yoru
to*] would make the above sentences correct:

天気予報によると、あしたは午後から大雨になるよう
　です。

*Tenki-yohō ni yoru to, ashita wa gogo kara ōame ni naru
   yō desu.*

According to the weather forecast, there should be heavy
   rain beginning tomorrow afternoon.

手紙によると、彼は来月結婚します。

*Tegami ni yoru to, kare wa raigetsu kekkon shimasu.*

According to the letter, he is getting married next month.

The connective によって [*ni yotte*] indicates the means
by which something is accomplished. In the following example, it shows how the speaker learned of the earthquake:

新聞<u>によって</u>、カリフォルニアに大きな地震があった
<u>ことを知った</u>。

*Shinbun <u>ni yotte</u>, Kariforunia ni ōkina jishin ga atta <u>koto
o shitta</u>.*

I found out from the newspaper that there was a big earthquake in California.

Another way to indicate hearsay is to use the dictionary
form of a verb followed by そうです [*sō desu*]. This pattern
is rather colloquial and more commonly used in conversation
and narration. For example:

明日の試験は中止する<u>そうです</u>。

*Asu no shiken wa chūshi suru <u>sō desu</u>.*

I hear that tomorrow's test is going to be cancelled.

In writing, という（ことである）[*to iu (koto de aru)*] and
と言われている [*to iwarete iru*] are more commonly used:

同国のスポークスマンによると核爆弾の使用を廃止す
る<u>ということである</u>。

*Dōkoku no supōkusuman ni yoru to kaku-bakudan no shiyō
o haishi suru <u>to iu koto de aru</u>.*

According to the country's spokesman, the use of nuclear
bombs will be banned.

昔はこの辺りの川でも砂金が採れた<u>と言われている</u>。

*Mukashi wa kono atari no kawa de mo sakin ga toreta <u>to
iwarete iru</u>.*

It is said that in the old days they were able to collect
gold dust even from the rivers in this area.

When the information source is a person, the formula is
usually A のはなしでは [*A no hanashi de wa*] or Aのはなし
だと [*A no hanashi da to*]:

ジムさんの<u>話だと</u>／<u>話では</u>、円が安くなったそうです
よ。

*Jimu-san no <u>hanashi da to</u> / <u>hanashi de wa</u>, en ga yasuku
natta sō desu yo.*

According to what Jim says, the yen has gone down.

As seen in the above example, this pattern is often used with
one of the hearsay endings, in this case そうだ [*sō da*].

---

- とか [*to ka*]

When とか [*to ka*] is used instead of と [*to*] as the particle of quotation, the quoted information is uncertain
or inexact. The speaker is not sure or does not remember the statement exactly.

明： 和子さん何て言ってた？
恵子： あした行く<u>とか</u>言ってたわよ。

*Akira: Kazuko-san nante itte 'ta?*
*Keiko: Ashita iku <u>to ka</u> itte 'ta wa yo.*

Akira: What did Kazuko say?
Keiko: She said she'll be going tomorrow or something like that.

---

# ■ Volition, Intention, Trial

### ➡ VERB まい（と思う）[*mai (to omou)*]

This pattern expresses the speaker's strong will *not* to do
something. The subject is in the first person.

我々は二度と戦争は起こすまいと誓った。

*Wareware wa nido to sensō wa okosu mai to chikatta.*

We vowed not to bring about a war ever again.

---

あんないやな人とはもう口をきくまいと思った。
*Anna iya na hito to wa mō kuchi o kiku mai to omotta.*
I made up my mind never to talk again to such a nasty person.

When the subject of the sentence is not the first person, まい [*mai*] is equivalent to 〜ないだろう [*~nai darō*] and means "probably not":

あんなに高い車は彼も買うまいと思っていたのだけれど、やはり買ったらしい。
*Anna ni takai kuruma wa kare mo kau mai to omotte ita no da keredo, yappari katta rashii.*
I thought that even he probably wouldn't buy an expensive car like that, but it seems he did buy it after all.

**➻ SENTENCE A 限り [*kagiri*] SENTENCE B**

In this pattern, sentence A indicates a condition or state and sentence B shows the speaker's strong intention or resolution.

健康である限りは働くぞと父が言った。
*Kenkō de aru kagiri wa hataraku zo to chichi ga itta.*
My father said, "As long as I am healthy, I will work."

私達は絶滅寸前の動物を救うため、できる限り努力すべきだ。
*Watashi-tachi wa zetsumetsu-sunzen mae no dōbutsu o sukuu tame, dekiru kagiri doryoku subeki da.*
We should try to do as much as we can to save endangered animals.

In the next sentence, the clause あの人が居る [*ano hito ga iru*] indicates an undesirable or inconvenient state:

あの人がいる限り、二度と行くまい（と思う）。

*Ano hito ga iru kagiri, nido to iku mai (to omou).*
As long as that person is there, I will never go again.

When the clause preceding 限り [*kagiri*] has a negative ending, it means "unless":

大雨が降らない限り、このダムは干上ってしまうだろう。
*Ōame ga furanai kagiri, kono damu wa hiagatte shimau darō.*
Unless there's a heavy rain, this dam will probably go dry.

社長が出席しない限り会議は始まらない。
*Shachō ga shusseki shinai kagiri kaigi wa hajimaranai.*
Unless the president attends, the meeting won't start.

## ➡ SENTENCE つもりだ [*tsumori da*]

This pattern expresses the speaker's intention, so the subject of つもりだ [*tsumori da*] should be "I" or "we":

一応行くつもりだけど……。
*Ichiō iku tsumori da kedo …*
I intend to go, but …

ちょっと忙しいから、今回は出席しないつもりです。
*Chotto isogashii kara, konkai wa shusseki shinai tsumori desu.*
I am a little busy, so I do not intend to attend this time.

When the sentence ending is in the past test, the truth is usually opposite to what is said in the sentence.

わたしもオーストラリアに行くつもりだったんです。
*Watashi mo Ōsutoraria ni iku tsumori datta n' desu.*
I was also planning to go to Australia (but I didn't go after all).

靴は買わないつもりだったのに、やっぱり買ってしまった。

*Kutsu wa kawanai tsumori datta no ni, yappari katte shimatta.*

I intended not to buy any shoes, but I ended up buying some.

When つもり [*tsumori*] is used after the -た [*-ta*] form of a verb, it often expresses the speaker's irritation:

今朝部屋をかたずけておきなさいって言ったつもりだけど……。

*Kesa heya o katazukete okinasai tte itta tsumori da kedo …*

I thought I told you this morning to clean up your room. (Why didn't you do it? Did you forget?)

---

• Pretending with つもり [*tsumori*]

The -たつもりだ [*-ta tsumori da*] pattern may also express a kind of play-acting on the speaker's part.

金がないから、今日はビールを飲んだつもりで早く帰ることにするよ。

*Kane ga nai kara, kyō wa bīru o nonda tsumori de hayaku kaeru koto ni suru yo.*

I don't have any money today, so I'll go home early, pretending that I did drink some beer.

---

The pattern つもりはない [*tsumori wa nai*] is more emphatic and shows the speaker's strong determination not to do something. するつもりはない [*suru tsumori wa nai*] is stronger than しないつもりだ [*shinai tsumori da*].

私は留学するつもりはない。

*Watashi wa ryūgaku suru tsumori wa nai.*
I have no intention to study abroad.

気 [*ki*] is sometimes used in place of つもり [*tsumori*] in this pattern:

この学生には全く勉強する気がないようだ。
*Kono gakusei ni wa mattaku benkyō suru ki ga nai yō da.*
This student seems to have no intention to study at all.

The pattern つもりじゃない／ではない [*tsumori ja nai / de wa nai*] means "I do not mean/intend ..." It is often used in apologies:

ごめんなさい。おどかすつもりじゃなかったんだけど
……。
*Gomen nasai. Odokasu tsumori ja nakatta n' da kedo ...*
I'm sorry. I didn't mean to scare you.

# ■ Subjunctive, Conditional: と／たら／ば／なら [to/tara/ba/nara]

This section presents the four basic patterns for expressing subjunctive and conditional concepts.

### ●◆ SENTENCE A と [*to*], SENTENCE B

The following are the basic patterns for the conditional と [*to*]:

VERB ⇨ VERB と [*to*].
ADJECTIVAL NOUN な [*na*] ⇨ ADJECTIVAL NOUN だと [*da to*]
NOUN ⇨ NOUN だと [*da to*]
ADJECTIVE ⇨ ADJECTIVE と [*to*]

行く ⇨ 行くと     *iku* ⇨ *iku to*
静かな ⇨ 静かだと     *shizuka na* ⇨ *shizuka da to*

明日 ⇨ 明日だと　　*asu* ⇨ *asu da to*
大きい ⇨ 大きいと　　*ōkii* ⇨ *ōkii to*

This と [*to*] expresses a repeated factual condition, a habitual occurrence, or an immediate sequence of events. Here are some examples of each:

✣ Repeated Factual Condition

毎年夏になると、この辺りはハイカーたちで賑わう。

*Maitoshi natsu ni naru to, kono atari wa haikā-tachi de nigiwau.*

When summer comes each year, this area becomes crowded with hikers.

大雨が降ると、あの川はよく氾濫する。

*Ōame ga furu to, ano kawa wa yoku hanran suru.*

When heavy rain falls, that river often floods over.

この坂を上り詰めると、よく海が見える。

*Kono saka o agaritsumeru to, yoku umi ga mieru.*

If you go up to the top of this slope, you can see the ocean quite well.

✣ Habitual Occurrence

京都に行くと、いつも嵯峨を訪れます

*Kyōto ni iku to, itsumo Saga o otozuremasu.*

Whenever I go to Kyoto, I always visit Saga.

あの人が入ると、いつもけんかになってしまう。

*Ano hito ga hairu to, itsumo kenka ni natte shimau.*

Whenever he joins in, we always end up arguing.

✣ Immediate Sequence of Events

彼は帰ると（すぐ）着替えてまた出かけた。

*Kare wa kaeru to (sugu) kigaete mata dekaketa.*

As soon as he came home, he changed his clothes and went out again.

次の角を右に曲がると、白い屋根の教会が見えます。

*Tsugi no kado o migi ni magaru to, shiroi yane no kyōkai ga miemasu.*

As soon as you turn right at the next corner, you'll see a church with a white roof.

---

- やいなや [*ya inaya*]

In writing, と（すぐ）[*to (sugu)*] may be replaced by やいなや [*ya inaya*]:

列車が停まるやいなや乗客がどっと乗りこんできた。

*Ressha ga tomaru ya inaya jōkyaku ga dotto norikon-de kita.*

As soon as the train halted, passengers came rushing in.

---

✧ *Set Phrases with* と [*to*]

÷A で言うと [*de iu to*]

In this pattern, A is an example or analogy.

ジル： 彼は、どんなタイプの人？

ショーン： 何って言ったらいいかな……。犬で言う
と、ボルゾイみたい。やせているけど、
背が高くて素敵な人。

*Jiru:*     *Kare wa, donna taipu no hito?*

*Shōn:*     *Nante ittara ii ka na … Inu de iu to, Boruzoi mitai. Yasete iru kedo, se ga takakute suteki na hito.*

Jill:      What type of person is he?

Shawn:     What should I say … If he were a dog, he'd
           be a borzoi. He's skinny, but tall and good-
           looking.

÷A で見ると [*de miru to*]、B

In this pattern, B is what the speaker learned from looking at A.

地図で見ると、日本は北東から南西に弓なりにつらな
った島国である。

*Chizu de miru to, Nihon wa hokutō kara nansei ni yumi-
nari ni tsuranatta shimaguni de aru.*

The map shows that Japan in an island country running
from northeast to southwest in the shape of a bow.

この写真で見ると犯人は若い男性らしい。

*Kono shashin de miru to hannin wa wakai dansei rashii.*

In this picture, the suspect seems to be a young man.

÷A からすると [*kara suru to*]、B

In this pattern, B is an inference or conjecture made by
the speaker based on A.

彼の嬉しそうな様子からすると試験に合格したようだ。

*Kare no ureshisō na yōsu kara suru to shiken ni gōkaku
shita yō da.*

Judging from his happy look, he seems to have passed the
examination.

÷A となると [*to naru to*]、B

Here, A refers to a hypothetical idea, and B is the result
or outcome of A.

今ヨーロッパに行くとなると、貯金を全部おろさなければならない。

*Ima Yōroppa ni iku to naru to, chokin o zenbu orosana-kereba naranai.*

If I go to Europe now, I'll have to withdraw all my savings.

✛ひょっとすると／もしかすると／ことによると [*hyotto suru to / moshi ka suru to / koto ni yoru to*]

These interchangeable expressions are often translated as "perhaps," "maybe," and "possibly." They show the speaker's wishful anticipation, strong hope, or fear and worry about something.

ひょっとすると、彼が迎えに来てくれるかもしれない。

*Hyotto suru to, kare ga mukae ni kite kureru ka mo shire-nai.*

It's just possible that he will come to pick me up.

もしかすると、今年は行けないかもしれない。

*Moshi ka suru to, kotoshi wa ikenai ka mo shirenai.*

I am afraid that I may not be able to go this year.

ことによると、奈良まで足を延ばすかもしれません。

*Koto ni yoru to, Nara made ashi o nobasu ka mo shire-masen.*

It is possible that I may extend my trip to Nara.

---

● 多分 [*tabun*]

多分 [*tabun*], "maybe, probably," is often used with expressions indicating uncertainty about the future. As shown by the following examples, the degree of uncertainty is determined by the context:

---

多分、今年は行けないかもしれない。
*Tabun, kotoshi wa ikenai ka mo shirenai.*
I may not be able to go there this year.

多分、今年は行けないだろう。
*Tabun, kotoshi wa ikenai darō.*
I probably won't be able to go there this year.

÷なぜかと言うと [*naze ka to iu to*]

This phrase indicates that the following sentence is an explanation for what came before. As in the next example, it can often be translated as "because":

わたしはあのデパートでは買物をしたくありません。
なぜかと言うと、二度もお財布をすられたことがあるからです。
*Watashi wa ano depāto de wa kaimono o shitaku arimasen. Naze ka to iu to, nido mo osaifu o surareta koto ga aru kara desu.*
I don't want to go shopping at that department store anymore, because I had my purse picked not once but twice there.

---

*Exercise 8* ———————————————————

Translate the following sentences into English.

1. 雨があがると、この谷に虹がかかる。
   *Ame ga agaru to, kono tani ni niji ga kakaru.*
2. あの上司は優しいけど怒ると、とても怖い。
   *Ano jōshi wa yasashii kedo donaru to, totemo kowai.*

3. テレビの音が大きすぎると、隣りから苦情が出る。
   *Terebi no oto ga ōkisugiru to, tonari kara kujō ga deru.*

4. 君も行くといいよ。とっても面白い映画だから。Ⓜ
   *Kimi mo iku to ii yo. Tottemo omoshiroi eiga da kara.*

5. 彼女は写真で見るとずいぶん老けて見えますね。
   *Kanojo wa shashin de miru to zuibun fukete miemasu ne.*

## ➥ SENTENCE A -たら [*-tara*], SENTENCE B

The following are the basic patterns for -たら [*-tara*]:

VERB -た ⇨ VERB -たら
    [*-ta*]        [*-tara*]
ADJECTIVAL NOUN な ⇨ ADJECTIVAL NOUN だったら
                [*na*]              [*dattara*]
NOUN ⇨ NOUN だったら
            [*dattara*]
ADJECTIVE -い ⇨ ADJECTIVE -かったら
            [*-i*]              [*-kattara*]

| 行った | ⇨ | 行ったら |
|---|---|---|
| [*itta*] | | [*ittara*] |
| 静かな | ⇨ | 静かだったら |
| [*shizuka na*] | | [*shizuka dattara*] |
| 明日 | ⇨ | 明日だったら |
| [*asu*] | | [*asu dattara*] |
| 大きい | ⇨ | 大きかったら |
| [*ōkii*] | | [*ōkikattara*] |

In an A-たら [*-tara*]、B sentence, A and B are not simultaneous or coexisting. The speaker is indicating that when A has actually occurred or is completed, B follows. For example:

マリーが来たらそう言っておきます。

*Marī ga kitara sō itte okimasu.*

When Marie comes, I'll tell her.

This -たら [-*tara*] pattern is similar in meaning to -た時に [-*ta toki ni*], -てから [-*te kara*], or -た後で [-*ta ato de*]. The following sentence has the same meaning as above:

マリーが来た時にそう言っておきます。

*Marī ga kita toki ni sō itte okimasu.*

When Marie comes, I'll tell her.

In these sentences, Marie's coming is not provisional or conditional. The speaker may not know exactly when Marie is coming, but at least the speaker knows that Marie will come.

Here are some more examples.

あしたマーケットに行ったら／行った時に、ミルクを
　買って。

*Ashita māketto ni ittara / itta toki ni, miruku o katte.*

Buy some milk when you go to the market tomorrow.

駅に着いたら／着いた時に、電話して。迎えに行くよ。

*Eki ni tsuitara / tsuita toki ni, denwa shite. Mukae ni iku yo.*

Call me when you get to the station. I'll come to pick you
　up.

雨が止んだら／止んでから、出かけよう。

*Ame ga yandara / yande kara, dekakeyō.*

Let's go (out) after the rain stops.

ビールを飲んだら／飲んだ後で、眠くなってしまった。

*Bīru o nondara / nonda ato de, nemuku natte shimatta.*

When I drank some beer, I got sleepy.

In the next two examples, the statement in the second half of the sentence is beyond the speaker's control, so only the -たら [-tara] form is possible:

熱が下がらなかったら、(出かけたくても) 出かけられない。

*Netsu ga sagaranakattara, (dekaketakute mo) dekakerare nai.*

(Even if I want to go out) I cannot go out unless my fever goes down.

これ以上雨が降ったら、川が氾濫する可能性がある。

*Kore ijō ame ga futtara, kawa ga hanran suru kanōsei ga aru.*

If the rain continues, there is the possibility that the river might overflow.

In the examples below, the first half of the sentence indicates what the speaker did intentionally or unintentionally, while the second half tells what the speaker discovered or realized. In this pattern, the second clause often ends with -ている／-ていた [-te iru / -te ita].

目を覚ましたら、もう夜が明けていた。

*Me o samashitara, mō yo ga akete ita.*

When I woke up, (I saw) it was already dawn.

電話をしたら、出かけた後だった。

*Denwa o shitara, dekaketa ato datta.*

When I called, (I found out that) he had already gone out.

調べてみたら、やはり偽物だった。

*Shirabete mitara, yahari nisemono datta.*

When I examined it, I saw that it was a fake after all.

気がついたら、お財布がなくなっていた。
*Ki ga tsuitara, osaifu ga nakunatte ita.*
I suddenly realized that my wallet was missing.

---

- Suggestions with -たら [*-tara*]

The -たら [*-tara*] form at the end of a sentence shows that the speaker is making a suggestion:

あなたも行ったら？
*Anata mo ittara?*
Why don't you go, too?

---

## ❖ SENTENCE A -ば [*-ba*], SENTENCE B

The ば [*ba*] ending indicates a hypothetical condition, possibility, etc.

The following are the -ば [*-ba*] forms of some common verbs and the verbs' potential forms.

| Dictionary Form | -ば [*-ba*] Form | -ば [*-ba*] Form of Potential |
|---|---|---|
| 食べる<br>*taberu* | 食べれば<br>*tabereba* | 食べられれば<br>*taberarereba* |
| くる<br>*kuru* | くれば<br>*kureba* | こられれば<br>*korarereba* |
| する<br>*suru* | すれば<br>*sureba* | できれば<br>*dekireba* |
| 会う<br>*au* | 会えば<br>*aeba* | 会えれば<br>*aereba* |
| 書く<br>*kaku* | 書けば<br>*kakeba* | 書ければ<br>*kakereba* |

| 泳ぐ | 泳げば | 泳げれば |
|---|---|---|
| *oyogu* | *oyogeba* | *oyogereba* |
| 話す | 話せば | 話せれば |
| *hanasu* | *hanaseba* | *hanasereba* |
| 立つ | 立てば | 立てれば |
| *tatsu* | *tateba* | *tatereba* |
| 死ぬ | 死ねば | 死ねれば |
| *shinu* | *shineba* | *shinereba* |
| 叫ぶ | 叫べば | 叫べれば |
| *sakebu* | *sakebeba* | *sakebereba* |
| 読む | 読めば | 読めれば |
| *yomu* | *yomeba* | *yomereba* |
| 降る | 降れば | (降れれば) |
| *oriru* | *orireba* | *orirereba* |

In the following example, the -ば [-ba] clause indicates a hypothetical concept:

雨が降れば、試合は中止になるだろう。
*Ame ga fureba, shiai wa chūshi ni naru darō.*
If it should rain, the game will probably be cancelled.

The adverbial もし [*moshi*] is often used in this pattern:

もしこれ以上円が高くなれば、日本には行けなくなる。
*Moshi kore ijō en ga takaku nareba, Nihon ni wa ikenaku naru.*
If the yen should get stronger, it will become impossible for me to go to Japan.

Sometimes the -ば [-ba] clause describes an existing state or fact that has already occurred. The speaker is using it as if it were a provisional condition. For example:

ここまで来れば、もう大丈夫。

*Koko made kureba, mō daijōbu.*

If we've come this far, then we must be safe.

In the following examples, the -なければ [-*nakereba*], meaning "if not," indicates something which contradicts a fact or reality. This type of sentence often takes the particle さえ [*sae*], which intensifies the previous word and the sentence-ending particle のに [*no ni*].

病気にさえならなければ、みんなと一緒に行けたのに。

*Byōki ni sae naranakereba, minna to issho ni iketa no ni.*

If only I hadn't become sick, I would have been able to go with everybody, but …

駅から遠くなければ、ここに住みたいけど。

*Eki kara tōku nakereba, koko ni sumitai kedo.*

If this place were closer to the station, I would like to live here, but …

It is also possible for the two parts of a -ば [-*ba*] sentence to have a cause-and-effect relationship or make a statement of fact. For example:

春が来れば、氷が溶けて花も咲き出す。

*Haru ga kureba, kōri ga tokete hana mo sakidasu.*

When spring comes, the ice melts and the flowers start to bloom.

Unlike the case of と [*to*], the first clause does not have to be a repeated factual condition. In the next example, the situation may be like this: the speaker and listener want to watch a parade, but there are so many people that they cannot see well. The speaker is suggesting that the listener go up to the second floor in order to get a better view. The -ば [-*ba*] clause—that is, 二階まで上がれば [*nikai made agareba*]—is the only condition that needs to be satisfied for the following clause—見える [*mieru*]—to become true.

二階まで上がれば、見える。
*Nikai made agareba, mieru.*
If you go up to the second floor, you will be able to see.

In the following proverb, the two halves of the sentence are not controlled by any time factor:

郷に入れば郷にしたがえ。
*Gō ni ireba gō ni shitagae.*
When you are in a village, do as the villagers do.
(When in Rome, do as the Romans do.)

When a ば [*ba*] clause is followed by a clause with も [*mo*], the two clauses indicate simultaneous or additional happenings or states. For example:

その宗教団体には、老人もいれば子供もいる。
*Sono shūkyō-dantai ni wa, rōjin mo ireba kodomo mo iru.*
In that religious group, there are old people and also children.

嵐も吹けば雨も降る。
*Arashi mo fukeba ame mo furu.*
The stormy wind blows and the rain falls.

**•• -なら (ば) [-*nara (ba)*]**

The following are the basic patterns for -なら [-*nara*]:

VERB ⇨ VERB -なら [-*nara*]
ADJECTIVAL NOUN な [*na*] ⇨ ADJECTIVAL NOUN なら [*nara*]
NOUN ⇨ NOUN なら [*nara*]

ADJECTIVE -い [-*i*] ⇨ ADJECTIVE -いなら [-*inara*]

行った [*itta*] ⇨ 行くなら [*iku nara*]
静かな [*shizuka na*] ⇨ 静かなら [*shizuka nara*]
先生 [*sensei*] ⇨ 先生なら [*sensei nara*]
高い [*takai*] ⇨ 高いなら [*takai nara*]

The -なら [-*nara*] clause is conditional. In other words, in A なら [-*nara*] B, A is the only condition for B to occur.

あしたなら、お手伝いできますけど……。
*Ashita nara, otetsudai dekimasu kedo ...*
If it is tomorrow, I will be able to help you (but not today).

君が来るなら、出かけずに待ってるよ。Ⓜ
*Kimi ga kuru nara, dekakezu ni matte 'ru yo.*
If you're coming, I won't go out. I'll wait for you.

In the last example above, for instance, the speaker may have planned on going out but changed his mind because the other person said that he would be coming.

---

• Origin of さようなら [*sayōnara*]

The Japanese greeting さようなら [*sayōnara*] contains the -なら [-*nara*] suffix. It originally meant "if it is so." The word suggests that the speaker does not want to be separated from the other person, but if their fate is to be separated, then the speaker must leave. Now that original meaning has been nearly forgotten, and さようなら [*sayōnara*] means only "good-bye."

### Exercise 9

Change each of the underlined verbs to the appropriate -と [-to], -たら [-tara], -ば [-ba], or -なら [-nara] form.

1. 母は銀座に<u>行く</u>（　　　　）いつもあの店で買い物をします。

   *Haha wa Ginza ni <u>iku</u> (　　　) itsumo ano mise de kaimono o shimasu.*

2. 花子さんから電話が<u>かかってくる</u>（　　　　）、二時ごろ居ると言って下さい。

   *Hanako-san kara denwa ga <u>kakatte kuru</u> (　　　), niji goro iru to itte kudasai.*

3. もし今大きな地震が<u>おきる</u>（　　　　）、このビルは崩壊してしまうにちがいない。

   *Moshi ima ōkina jishin ga <u>okiru</u> (　　　), kono biru wa hōkai shite shimau ni chigai nai.*

4. あの人がパーティーに<u>来る</u>（　　　　）、わたしは絶対に行かない。

   *Ano hito ga pātī ni <u>kuru</u> (　　　), watashi wa zettai ni ikanai.*

5. 今100ドル<u>もっている</u>（　　　　）何に使いますか。

   *Ima hyaku-doru <u>motte iru</u> (　　　) nani ni tsukaimasu ka.*

6. そんな事をする暇が<u>ある</u>（　　　　）、少しは勉強しなさいよ。

   *Sonna koto o suru hima ga <u>aru</u> (　　　), sukoshi wa benkyō shinasai yo.*

7. もし<u>できる</u>（　　　　）、一緒に行っていただきたいんですけど……。

*Moshi <u>dekiru</u> (          ), issho ni itte itadakitai n'
desu kedo ...*

8. <u>見えない</u> (          )、もっと前の方に座ったら。
   *<u>Mienai</u> (          ), motto mae no hō ni suwattara.*

9. <u>おいしくない</u> (          )、食べなくてもいいんですよ。
   *<u>Oishiku nai</u> (          ), tabenakute mo ii n' desu yo.*

10. 味が<u>うすい</u> (          )、おしょうゆをもう少し入れ
    てね。
    *Aji ga <u>usui</u> (          ), oshōyu o mō sukoshi irete ne.*

## ■ Time-related Expressions

### ●◆ When: SENTENCE A 時 (に) [*toki (ni)*]、SENTENCE B

While one meaning of the noun 時 [*toki*] is "time," when it comes after a clause or other modifier it usually means "when."

In English, the tense of subordinate clauses must agree with the tense of the main clause, while in Japanese there is no such agreement of tense. This difference often creates problems for students. In Japanese, the tense is indicated only by the main verb. Other verb endings merely tell relative time.

When the subordinate verb before 時 [*toki*] is in the non-past (dictionary) form, it indicates that the action of the verb is not yet completed. Consider the next three examples:

(a) おすしを<u>食べる</u>時には、お箸は使わなくてもいい。
   *Osushi o <u>taberu</u> toki ni wa, ohashi wa tsukawanakute mo ii.*
   When you eat sushi, you don't have to use chopsticks.

(b) ここに<u>来る</u>時スーザンの所に寄って来た。

*Koko ni <u>kuru</u> toki Sūzan no tokoro ni yotte kita.*

When I was coming here, I dropped by Susan's house.

(c) <u>寝る</u>時に電気を消して下さい。

*<u>Neru</u> toki ni denki o keshite kudasai.*

Please turn off the light when you go to bed.

In (a), the verb 食べる [*taberu*] refers to the process of eating without mentioning a particular time. In (b), the action of 来る [*kuru*] was not yet completed when the speaker dropped by at Susan's house. And in (c), the listener is supposed to turn off the light before going to bed at some point in the future. In each case, the verb's action is incomplete, so the verb is in the nonpast form.

When the action of the verb is completed, then the past form is used. For example:

(d) きのうここに<u>来た</u>時にペンを忘れて行ったと思うんだけど、見かけなかった？

*Kinō koko ni <u>kita</u> toki ni pen o wasurete itta to omou n' da kedo mikakenakatta?*

I think I left my pen when I came here yesterday. Did you happen to see it?

(e) カメラは今度日本に<u>行った</u>時に買います。

*Kamera wa kondo Nihon ni <u>itta</u> toki ni kaimasu.*

I'll buy a camera in Japan the next time I go.

In (d), the action of 来た [*kita*] was finished when the speaker forgot her pen, so the past form is used. Similarly, in (e) the speaker will have completed going to Japan when he buys a camera, and that completed action is indicated by the past form 行った [*itta*].

- Tense of Verb

When the clause before 時 [*toki*] describes a state rather than an action, the clause's verb may take either the nonpast ending or past ending:

日本にいる時に、よくお相撲を見に行った。
*Nihon ni iru toki ni, yoku osumō o mi ni itta.*
日本にいた時に、よくお相撲を見に行った。
*Nihon ni ita toki ni, yoku osumō o mi ni itta.*
When I was in Japan, I often went to see sumō.

- Replacements for 時 [*toki*]

In writing and formal speech, 際 [*sai*] or 折 [*ori*] may be used in place of 時 [*toki*]. The expression -にあたって [*-ni atatte*] "at the time of" is also used in a formal speech, though it would sound awkward in everyday conversation.

出発にあたって、一言ご挨拶申し上げます。
*Shuppatsu ni atatte, hitokoto go-aisatsu mōshiage-masu.*
At this time of my departure, I would like to say a few words.

この問題は、今日の会議の際に取り上げることになっている。
*Kono mondai wa, kyō no kaigi no sai ni toriageru koto ni natte iru.*
This issue is to be discussed at today's meeting.

日本を出ます折には 色々お世話になりました。

*Nihon o demasu ori ni wa iroiro o-sewa ni narima-shita.*

Thank you for your help and concern at the time of my going abroad.

●◆ **Just As: SENTENCE A** -たとたんに **[-*ta totan ni*]、 SENTENCE B**

The connective とたん [*totan*] indicates that the actions of sentences A and B are nearly simultaneous. The preceding verb is in the -た [-*ta*] form.

As in the first example below, the main verb of the clause preceding とたん [*totan*] may be the volitional form, followed by -とした [-*to shita*].

大好きなパイを食べようとしたとたんに目が覚めてしまった。

*Daisuki na pai o tabeyō to shita totan ni me ga samete shimatta.*

Just as I was about to eat a piece of my favorite pie, I woke up.

わたしが乗ったとたんに、バスが発車した。

*Watashi ga notta totan ni, basu ga hassha shita.*

The bus left just as I got on.

とたんに [*totan ni*] may be replaced by ところで [*tokoro de*] or ところに [*tokoro ni*], but with these connectives the focus is on the situation or state rather than the moment itself:

寝ようとしたところに、電話がかかって来た。

*Neyō to shita tokoro ni, denwa ga kakatte kita.*
As I was going to bed, there was a telephone call.

私が話そうとしたところで、時間切れになってしまった。
*Watashi ga hanasō to shita tokoro de, jikan-gire ni natte shimatta.*
As I was about to speak, time ran out.

●● **While:** 間／間は／間に／-ながら [*aida / aida wa / aida ni / -nagara*]

The concept "while" can be expressed by 間 [*aida*] or the verb suffix -ながら [*-nagara*].

Like 時 [*toki*], the word 間 [*aida*] is a noun, and so the clause preceding it is a noun modifier.

The two clauses connected by 間 [*aida*] must have the same time duration and be concurrent. For example:

日本にいる間、できるだけ日本語で話します。
*Nihon ni iru aida, dekiru dake Nihongo de hanashimasu.*
While I am in Japan, I'll speak in Japanese as much as possible.

子供が寝ている間、静かにしていてください。
*Kodomo ga nete iru aida, shizuka ni shite ite kudasai.*
While the children are sleeping, please keep quiet.

When 間 [*aida*] is replaced by 間は [*aida wa*], the speaker is implying that when the action of the first clause is completed, the action of the second clause may be discontinued.

子供が寝ている間は、静かにしていて下さい。
*Kodomo ga nete iru aida wa, shizuka ni shite ite kudasai.*
While the children are sleeping, please keep quiet. (After they wake up, you may make noise).

The connective 間 に [*aida ni*] indicates that the two clauses overlap only partially. For example:

日本にいる間に、中国に遊びに行くつもりだ。
*Nihon ni iru aida ni, Chūgoku ni asobi ni iku tsumori da.*
While I am in Japan, I am planning to visit China.

Only 間に [*aida ni*] is possible in this case. A sentence like 日本にいる間、中国に遊びに行くつもりだ [*Nihon ni iru aida, Chūgoku ni asobi ni iku tsumori da*] would be impossible, because it would suggest that the speaker will be in China for the entire time of his stay in Japan.

Another way to say "while" is with the verb suffix -なが ら [*-nagara*], which attaches to the stem of the -ます [*-masu*] form of the verb. Keep in mind that 間 [*aida*] and -ながら [*-nagara*] are not interchangeable. For example, the following sentence is inappropriate:

わたしは、歩きながら先生に会った。
*Watashi wa, arukinagara sensei ni atta.*
While I was walking, I saw my teacher.

The -ながら [*-nagara*] is used to indicate that one person or group is doing two or more things simultaneously and intentionally. The example immediately above is inappropriate, because to see someone on the way is not intentional, but co-incidental.

In the case of 間 [*aida*] (or 間は [*aida wa*] or 間に [*aida ni*]), the subject of the two clauses can be different. With -なが ら [*-nagara*], though, the subjects must be the same. In other words, -ながら [*-nagara*] is used to indicate that one person or group is doing two or more things at the same time.

私は本を読みながら、よく音楽を聞く。
*Watashi wa hon o yominagara, yoku ongaku o kiku.*

I often listen to music while I'm reading.

**⇥ Before:** 前（に）／〜ないうちに [*mae (ni)* / *~nai uchi ni*]

The word 前 [*mae*] expresses the concept "before."

Like 時 [*toki*] and 間 [*aida*], 前 [*mae*] is a noun, so it can be preceded by a modifying clause. The verb of that preceding clause is always in the nonpast form.

When the particle に [*ni*] follows 前 [*mae*], it refers to a particular point in time, just as in phrases like 一時に [*ichiji ni*] "at one o'clock," 日曜日に [*nichiyōbi ni*] "on Sunday," or 家を出る時に [*ie o deru toki ni*] "(at the point in time) when I go out."

> ここに来る前、ドイツに住んでいました。
> *Koko ni kuru mae, Doitsu ni sunde imashita.*
> Before I came here, I lived in Germany.

> 寝る前に、歯をみがきなさい。
> *Neru mae ni, ha o migakinasai.*
> Brush your teeth before you go to sleep.

Another way to say "before" is with the negative (-ない [*-nai*]) form of a verb followed by うちに [*uchi ni*]. Compare the following:

(a) 雨が<u>ひどくなる前</u>に、帰った方がいい。
    *Ame ga <u>hidoku naru mae ni</u>, kaetta hō ga ii.*

(b) 雨が<u>ひどくならないうちに</u>、帰った方がいい。
    *Ame ga <u>hidoku naranai uchi ni</u>, kaetta hō ga ii.*

Both (a) and (b) mean "you'd better go home before it starts pouring." However, there is a difference in nuance. Sentence (a) is a simple suggestion, while (b) expresses the speaker's concern and worry for the other person. In other words, A -な

いうちに [-*nai uchi ni*] sentences imply that there will be a problem if A happens.

### ❖ YEAR/MONTH/etc. に入って [*ni haitte*]

The expression X に入って [*ni haitte*] literally means "entered X and…" The X in this formula must be a specific time period, such as a month, year, era, vacation, etc. This expression is more commonly used in writing to indicate a change or shift in time. Some examples:

九月に入って、やっと涼しくなって来ました。
*Kugatsu ni haitte, yatto suzushiku natte kimashita.*
It finally started to get cooler beginning in early September.

明治時代に入って、だれでも教育が受けられるように
なった。
*Meiji jidai ni haitte, dare de mo kyōiku ga ukerareru yō ni natta.*
In the early Meiji Period, it became possible for anyone to receive an education.

## ■ Disappointment, Annoyance, Regret ──────

### ❖ VERB -てしまう [-*te shimau*] ／ VERB -れる [-*reru*]

This section describes two patterns for expressing disappointment, annoyance, or regret.

In the first pattern, the -て [-*te*] form of the verb is followed by the verb しまう [*shimau*]. This pattern indicates that the speaker is upset or disappointed about what has happened. For example:

駅でアンに会ってしまった。
*Eki de An ni atte shimatta.*

(I was hoping not to see her, but) I ran into Anne at the station.

彼は行ってしまった。
*Kare wa itte shimatta.*
He's gone. (I'm sad, and I miss him!)

The second pattern uses the passive form of the verb. In this case, the passive indicates that the incident caused the speaker to suffer emotionally, financially, physically, etc. This is usually called the "adverse passive" (see page 131). Here are two examples:

父に死なれたために働きに出なければならなかった。
*Chichi ni shinareta tame ni hataraki ni denakereba naranakatta.*
I had to get a job because my father died.

夕べ夜おそく電話をかけられたので、今朝は眠い。
*Yūbe yoru-osoku denwa o kakerareta no de, kesa wa nemui.*
Someone called me late last night, so I am sleepy this morning.

Note that these two patterns are not interchangeable. While -てしまう [-*te shimau*] indicates only that the speaker is upset about the action of the verb, the passive form says that the speaker has actually suffered as a result. Students often make the wrong choice and say, for example, 駅でアンに会われました [*Eki de An ni awaremashita*]. The correct expression should be, as shown above, 駅でアンに会ってしまった [*Eki de An ni atte shimatta*].

- Passive Forms of Verbs

Irregular Verbs

| | |
|---|---|
| 来る ⇨ 来られる | *kuru ⇨ korareru* |
| する ⇨ される | *suru ⇨ sareru* |

Vowel-Stem Verbs

| | |
|---|---|
| 食べる ⇨ 食べられる | *taberu ⇨ taberareru* |
| いる ⇨ いられる | *iru ⇨ irareru* |

Consonant-Stem Verbs

| | |
|---|---|
| 会う ⇨ 会われる | *au ⇨ awareru* |
| 書く ⇨ 書かれる | *kaku ⇨ kakareru* |
| 話す ⇨ 話される | *hanasu ⇨ hanasareru* |
| 立つ ⇨ 立たれる | *tatsu ⇨ tatareru* |
| 死ぬ ⇨ 死なれる | *shinu ⇨ shinareru* |
| 呼ぶ ⇨ 呼ばれる | *yobu ⇨ yobareru* |
| 読む ⇨ 読まれる | *yomu ⇨ yomareru* |
| 降る ⇨ 降られる | *furu ⇨ furareru* |

# ■Tendency: きらいがある, がちだ [kirai ga aru, gachi da]

➥ **A は [*wa*] SENTENCE B きらいがある [*kirai ga aru*]**

This pattern says that A has an undesirable tendency to behave as described in B. The undesirable behavior is usually intentional, and A uses this expression to warn the listener:

あの人は話を誇張するきらいがあるから気をつけて聞いた方がいい。

*Ano hito wa hanashi o kochō suru kirai ga aru kara ki o tsukete kiita hō ga ii.*

You'd better be careful about what he says, because he
  tends to exaggerate.

あの会社は手ぬき工事をするきらいがある。
*Ano kaisha wa tenuki kōji o suru kirai ga aru.*
That company tends to do sloppy work.

**•❖ A は [*wa*] NOUN/VERB がちだ [*gachi da*] or NOUN/VERB
がちの [*gachi no*] A**

The suffix -がち [*-gachi*] indicates A's physical or emotional
tendency. The suffix may also indicate that the speaker feels
sympathy toward the subject of the sentence.

-がち [*-gachi*] is used after descriptive nouns and after
verbs in the pre-ます [*-masu*] form.

母は病気がちなので、あまり外には出ないのです。
*Haha wa byōki-gachi na no de, amari soto ni wa denai
  no desu.*
My mother is not very healthy (lit., tends to get sick), so
  she usually stays home (lit., does not go out very often.)

六月にはいると、雨がちの日が続く。
*Rokugatsu ni hairu to, ame-gachi no hi ga tsuzuku.*
Rainy weather will continue in June.

# MISCELLANEOUS
# CONNECTIONS

## ■ として [toshite]

### ◦ Noun として [*toshite*]

In this pattern, として [*toshite*] is usually translated as "as":

> 彼は留学性として日本に行ったことがある。
> *Kare wa ryūgakusei toshite Nihon ni itta koto ga aru.*
> He has been to Japan as a foreign (study-abroad) student.

> 市民の一人として、市の政策に怒りを感ずる。
> *Shimin no hitori toshite, shi no seisaku ni ikari o kanzuru.*
> As a city resident, I feel resentment against the policies of
>    the city government.

### ◦ Sentence (もの)として [*(mono) toshite*]

Here, として [*toshite*] indicates an assumption:

> A: あすのパーティーの飲み物はどの位用意したらい
>    いかしら。
> B: さあ、みんな来るものとして50人分用意した方が
>    いいんじゃないかな。
> *A: Asu no pātī no nomimono wa dono kurai yōi shitara ii*
>    *kashira.*
> *B: Sā, minna kuru mono toshite gojū-nin bun yōi shita hō*
>    *ga ii n' ja nai ka na.*
> A: I wonder how many drinks we should prepare for to-
>    morrow's party?

B: Well, wouldn't it be safer to prepare for 50 people, assuming everybody is coming?

### ➻ Noun としては [*toshite wa*]

This pattern puts extra focus on the sentence topic. It often indicates that the rest of the sentence concerns only that topic or aspect and that other possible topics or aspects might be different.

> わたくしとしては、こんなことは言いたくないのですが……。
>
> *Watakushi toshite wa, konna koto wa iitakunai no desu ga ...*
>
> As for me, I don't want to say this, but ...

> 子供が画いたものとしてはすばらしいできですね。
>
> *Kodomo ga egaita mono toshite wa subarashii deki desu ne.*
>
> For a child's drawing, this is excellent work.

### ➻ N としても [*toshite mo*]

This pattern indicates that the topic noun shares with others what is indicated in the rest of the sentence.

> 私としても、彼女のきたないやり方にはうんざりしています。
>
> *Watashi toshite mo, kanojo no kitanai yarikata ni wa unzari shite imasu.*
>
> I, too, am disgusted by her underhanded ways.

### ■ 今にも, 今だに [ima ni mo, imada ni]

### ➻ 今にも〜そうだ [*ima ni mo ~sō da*]

This pattern expresses the idea that, based on the speaker's observation, something is on the verge of happening.

今にも雨が降り出しそうな空。

*Ima ni mo ame ga furidashisō na sora.*

Looks like it might start raining any minute now.

女の子は今にも泣き出しそうな顔していた。

*Onna no ko wa ima ni mo nakidashisō na kao shite ita.*

The girl looked as if she were going to burst into tears at any moment.

**➻ いまだに [*imada ni*]**

This expression means "even now" or "still." It often has a mildly negative connotation.

私にはいまだにあの人の気持ちが分からない。

*Watashi ni wa imada ni ano hito no kimochi ga wakaranai.*

(Even now) I still don't understand how she feels.

ハイウエーの工事はいまだに終わっていない。

*Haiwē no kōji wa imada ni owatte inai.*

The highway construction has still not been completed.

# ■ それから, その上 [sore kara, sono ue], and それに [sore ni]

**➻ SENTENCE A, それから [*sore kara*] SENTENCE B**

それから [*sore kara*] shows the sequence of events that are somehow related. It is often translated as "and then."

感謝祭には親戚の者達が家に集まって料理をします。それからごちそうを食べたり歌をうたったりします。

*Kansha-sai ni wa shinseki no monotachi ga ie ni atsumatte ryōri o shimasu. Sore kara gochisō o tabetari uta o utattari shimasu.*

At Thanksgiving, our relatives gather at our home and cook a meal, and then we eat the food, sing songs, and do other things.

**••> SENTENCE A,** その上／それに *[sono ue / sore ni]* **SENTENCE B**

These patterns are used to give additional information. Unlike それから *[sore kara]*, they do not specify the order of events.

> これはあまり新鮮ではありません。そのうえ、高すぎます。(だから買うのはやめます。)
>
> *Kore wa amari shinsen de wa arimasen. Sono ue, taka-sugimasu. (Da kara kau no wa yamemasu.)*
>
> This is not very fresh, and it is too expensive. (So I am not going to buy it.)

> ちょっと疲れているの。それに雨も降っているから、今日は失礼するわ。
>
> *Chotto tsukarete iru no. Sore ni ame mo futte iru kara, kyō wa shitsurei suru wa.*
>
> I'm a little tired. In addition to that, it's raining, so please excuse me today.

## ■ 強いて言えば *[shiite ieba]*

This expression, which literally means "if I am forced to say," is used when one is reluctantly giving an opinion or having difficulty determining the right answer or opinion. It is often preceded by a condition or reservation.

> その件についてはあまり意見がないのですが、強いて言えば、検察側の見方がちょっと甘かったような気がします。
>
> *Sono ken ni tsuite wa amari iken ga nai no desu ga, shiite*

*ieba, kensatsu-gawa no mikata ga chotto amakatta yō
na ki ga shimasu.*

I don't have much of an opinion about the case. If anything, I feel that the prosecutor's view was a little too optimistic.

# ■The Uses of 人 [hito]

Sentences like the following are common in student compositions:

クリスマスには、人たちが集まってキリストの誕生を
祝います.

*Kurisumasu ni wa, hito-tachi ga atsumatte Kirisuto no
tanjō o iwaimasu.*

On Christmas Day, people gather and celebrate the birth of Jesus Christ.

The たち [tachi] is a plural marker for people, so 人たち [hito-tachi] sounds correct to English speakers. It is, however, inappropriate and awkward here. Only when 人たち [hito-tachi] is specified by noun modifiers or demonstratives (i.e., この [kono] or その [sono]) can it appear in sentences of this sort. Here, 人々 [hitobito] should be used instead of 人たち [hito-tachi].

The following two examples are correct:

最近の若い人たちの間では、どんなヘアスタイルがは
やっているんですか。

*Saikin no wakai hito-tachi no aida de wa, donna heasu-
tairu ga hayatte iru n' desu ka.*

What kinds of hair styles are popular among young people these days?

あの人たちはどこからやって来たのだろうか。

*Ano hito-tachi wa doko kara yatte kita no darō ka.*
I wonder where those people came from?

The word 人 [*hito*] may mean either a person or people in general, as in 世界の人 [*sekai no hito*] "people of the world," but it may also be used in place of "I" (わたし [*watashi*], ぼく [*boku*], etc.) when the speaker wants to complain about someone else without sounding harsh. For example:

人の言うこともすこしは聞いたらどうなの。
*Hito no iu koto mo sukoshi wa kiitara dō na no.*
Can't you pay a little attention to what a person is saying?

人の前をうろうろしないでよ。気がちるから。
*Hito no mae o urouro shinai de yo. Ki ga chiru kara.*
Stop walking around in front of me. I can't concentrate.

なんでもかんでも人に押し付けないでよ。わたしも忙しいんだから……。
*Nandemo-kandemo hito ni oshitsukenai de yo. Watashi mo isogashii n' da ka ra ...*
Don't make me do everything! I am busy, too, you know.

# ■ Passive and Causative

## ●◆ -られる/-れる [-*rareru*/-*reru*] Passive

### A. Regular

The -られる/-れる [-*rareru*/-*reru*] form corresponds to the passive voice in English. In an active sentence, the agent of the verb—that is, the person or thing doing the action of the verb—is also the subject, and the patient—the recipient of the verb's action—is the direct object. In a passive sentence, the roles are reversed; the patient becomes the subject, and the agent is shown as an oblique phrase with に [*ni*] or omitted entirely.

In Japanese, the passive voice is common in impersonal writing like newspaper articles and reports. In such sentences, the focus is on what was done or what happened, not on who or what did it. Consequently, the agent is often deleted when unknown or when understood from the context.

In the first example, the agent is unknown:

見なれぬ車が乗り捨てられている。

*Minarenu kuruma ga norisuterarete iru.*

An unfamiliar car has been abandoned.

In the next example, the agent is understood to be the Japanese people:

日本では、一般にお米が主食として食べられている。

*Nihon de wa, ippan ni o-kome ga shushoku toshite taberarete iru.*

In Japan, rice is usually eaten as the staple food.

## B. Adversative

Another use of -られる／-れる [*-rareru/-reru*] is the "adversative." Native speakers of Japanese commonly use the adversative -られる／-れる [*-rareru/-reru*] to express displeasure or distress without mentioning it explicitly. Adverbs such as "unfortunately" or "too bad" may be added to the English translation to suggest the feeling of adversity. When the verb is transitive, the agent becomes an oblique phrase marked with に [*ni*], while the direct object, marked with を [*o*], is unchanged. Compare the following active and passive sentences:

(a) あの男が少年の財布をすった。

　　*Ano otoko ga shōnen no saifu o sutta.*

　　That man stole the boy's wallet.

(b) 少年はあの男に財布をすられた。

*Shōnen wa ano otoko ni saifu o surareta.*

The boy had his wallet stolen by that man.

In (b), the passive verb すられた [*surareta*] indicates that the boy was affected adversely by the man's act of stealing. The one who caused the trouble is marked by に [*ni*].

It is also possible to form the adverse passive with intransitive verbs. This pattern is very commonly used to suggest distress, disappointment, or sadness. Such sentences can often be translated as active sentences with adverbs such as "unfortunately" or "too bad." For example:

大雪に降られて、交通がまひした。

*Ōyuki ni furarete, kōtsū ga mahi shita.*

Heavy snow fell (unfortunately), and traffic was paralyzed.

待望の旅行だったのに，雨に降られて駄目になってしまった。

*Taibō no ryokō datta no ni, ame ni furarete dame ni natte shimatta.*

Although it was a long-awaited trip, it became impossible because of the rain (lit., because the rain fell).

C. Spontaneous: -ものと思われる／考えられる／感じられる etc. [-*mono to omowareru/kangaerareru/kanjirareru*]

This -*rareru* pattern is often used by native speakers of Japanese to make a statement hypothetical, tentative, or indefinite, in order to avoid making an irrevocable commitment. Although this use of -*rareru* is an important part of Japanese communication strategies, it is not included in most Japanese textbooks. Translations such as "It is thought that" and "one may think that" for *omowarereru,* for example, are included without any explanation. The -*rareru* indicates that the subject of the sentence is not intentionally or actively involved in the thinking and perceiving. It suggests that an idea or feeling has spontaneously and naturally come to mind. In other words, such an idea or feeling is not the result of someone's actions, but a spontaneous occurrence.

このような傾向は 今後も強くなるものと思われます.

*Kono yō na keikō wa kongo mo tsuyoku naru mono to omowaremasu.*

It seems to me that this sort of trend may become stronger from now on.

## D. Honorifics

This -られる [*-rareru*] pattern is used to show respect. Compared with other honorific forms, the -られる／れる [*-rareru/ -reru*] honorifics appear to be more commonly used by male speakers.

先生はいつ帰られますか。

*Sensei wa itsu kaeraremasu ka.*

When will the teacher come back?

## ●◆ -せる／-させる [*-seru / -saseru*] (Causative)

The -せる/-させる [*-seru/-saseru*] form is usually called the causative, but it is also used to give permission. The following example uses a transitive verb. Note the use of particles.

先生が 学生に本を読ませた。

*Sensei ga gakusei ni hon o yomaseta.*

The teacher made the students read the book.

When the verb is intransitive, the one who actually performs the action or motion is usually marked by に [*ni*] when the meaning is causative and by を [*o*] in the case of permission. Compare the following:

子供に行かせる。
*Kodomo ni ikaseru.*
I make my child go.

子供を行かせる。
*Kodomo o ikaseru.*
I let my child go.

### ➡ -させられる／-せられる or -される [*-saserareru/-sera-reru/-sareru*] Causative-Passive

The pattern is usually called Causative-Passive. It indicates that the subject is forced to do something, or is doing something reluctantly. There are verbs with -す [*-su*] endings that have causative meanings, so the Causative-Passive is not -せられた [*-serareta*] but -された [*-sareta*].

私は友達に納豆を食べさせられた。
*Watashi wa tomodachi ni nattō o tabesaserareta.*
I was forced to eat *natto* by my friend.

Note the use of particles. The one who is forced to do or is reluctant to do the action is the subject of the sentence, and the one who causes the inconvenience is marked by に [*ni*].

## ■Noun を [o] Verb する [suru]／Noun の [no] Noun をする [o suru]

A common mistake among beginning Japanese students is to say 日本語を勉強をする [*Nihongo o benkyō o suru*]. This sentence should be either of the following:

(a) 日本語を勉強する。

*Nihongo o benkyō suru.*

(b) 日本語の勉強をする。

*Nihongo no benkyō o suru.*

There are many *kango* (Chinese compounds or Chinese loanwords) in Japanese that can take する [*suru*] and function as verbs. In the above sentences, 勉強 [*benkyō*] is a noun and 勉強する [*benkyō suru*] is a verb. Accordingly, 勉強する [*benkyō suru*] takes 日本語 [*Nihongo*] as the object in (a), while in (b) 勉強 [*benkyō*] becomes the object of する [*suru*], and 日本語 [*nihongo*] modifies 勉強 [*benkyō*].

---

- Only One Direct Object

A verb can take only one direct object in a sentence. That is why 日本語を勉強をする [*Nihongo o benkyō o suru*] is awkward.

---

Here are some more examples.

辞書を改訂する
*jisho o kaitei suru*
to revise a dictionary

辞書の改訂をする
*jisho no kaitei o suru*
to make a revision of a dictionary

うちの会社では外車は販売していない。
*Uchi no kaisha de wa gaisha wa hanbai shite inai.*
Our company does not sell foreign cars.

うちの会社では外車の販売をしていない。
*Uchi no kaisha de wa gaisha no hanbai o shite inai.*

Our company does not undertake the sale of foreign cars.

## ■-ておいて [-te oite]

As discussed in the -て [-te] form section (see page 59), -て [-te] plus おく [oku] usually means that the action or motion is carried out ahead of time for future use or as a favor for another person. For example:

今晩、友だちが来るからビールを買っておこう。
*Konban, tomodachi ga kuru kara bīru o katte okō.*
Some friends are coming over tonight, so I'll buy some beer (in advance).

The -ておいて [-te oite] ending can also suggest disgusted or resentful feelings:

彼女はさんざん迷惑をかけておいて、謝ろうともしない。
*Kanojo wa sanzan meiwaku o kakete oite, ayamarō to mo shinai.*
Although she's really been a bother, she doesn't even try to apologize.

This -ておいて [-te oite] is often interchangeable with -ておきながら[-te okinagara], -たのに [-ta no ni], or -たにもかかわらず [-ta ni mo kakawarazu]. The sentence above can thus become either of the following:

彼女はさんざん迷惑をかけたのに謝ろうともしない。
*Kanojo wa sanzan meiwaku o kaketa no ni ayamarō to mo shinai.*

彼女はさんざん迷惑をかけたにもかかわらず謝ろうともしない。
*Kanojo wa sanzan meiwaku o kaketa ni mo kakawarazu ayamarō to mo shinai.*

Here is another example of -ておいて [*-te oite*]:

あれだけの大罪をおかしておいて、まだ無罪を主張するなんて……。

*Aredake no taizai o okashite oite, mada muzai o shuchō suru nante ...*

It's hard to believe that he insists on pleading not guilty even after committing such a heinous crime.

# ■ Uses of になる [ni naru]

The phrase になる [*ni naru*] has several meanings. One is "to become":

私は将来、海洋学者になりたい。
*Watashi wa shōrai, kaiyōgaku-sha ni naritai.*
I want to become an oceanographer in the future.

になる [*ni naru*] can also mean "to attain an age":

好子は来月二十になります。
*Yoshiko wa raigetsu hatachi ni narimasu.*
Yoshiko will turn twenty next month.

Another meaning of になる [*ni naru*] is "to reach a total." While 百円です [*hyaku-en desu*] may tell the price of one item, 百円になります [*hyaku-en ni narimasu*] tells the total price of several items. For example:

(梨は三つで) 六百円になります。
*(Nashi wa mittsu de) roppyaku-en ni narimasu.*
The total (price) (for three pears) is 600 yen.

(全部で) 100ページぐらいになると思います。
*(Zenbu de) hyaku-pēji gurai ni naru to omoimasu.*
I think the total will be about 100 pages.

• Meaning of で [*de*]

In sentences such as Xは百円です [*X wa hyaku-en desu*] "X is ¥100" or Xは百円します [*X wa hyaku-en shimasu*] "X costs ¥100," X can be one object or several. When the particle で [*de*] is used instead of は [*wa*], though, X cannot be a single object; it must be more than one. In such cases, になります [*ni narimasu*] may replace です [*desu*] or します [*shimasu*]. For example:

これはいくらだったの?
*Kore wa ikura datta no?*
How much were these? / How much was this?

これで10ドルです／になります。
*Kore de jū-doru desu / ni narimasu.*
The total price for these will be $10.

## ■ ということです [to iu koto desu]────────

This sentence ending can be used to report something that was heard from someone else:

山田さんからお電話がありました。あす十時にこちら
にいらっしゃると言うことです。
*Yamada-san kara o-denwa ga arimashita. Asu jū-ji ni kochira ni irassharu to iu koto desu.*
You had a phone call from Ms. Yamada. She said that she would come here at ten o'clock tomorrow.

ということです [*to iu koto desu*] is also used to give explanations. In this sense, it is a replacement for といういみ です [*to iu imi desu*]:

A: (ということは) あなたは行かないということですね。

B: ちがいます。行きますけどみんなと一緒には行けないということです。

A: *(To iu koto wa) anata wa ikanai to iu koto desu ne.*

B: *Chigaimasu. Ikimasu kedo minna to issho ni wa ikenai to iu koto desu.*

A: (So you are saying that) this means that you are not going, right?

B: No. It means that I can go but that I can't go together with everyone else.

## ■ VERB -ぬうちに [-nu uchi ni]/VERB -ないうちに [-nai uchi ni]

As mentioned on page 120, a negative (-ない [-*nai*]) verb followed by うちに [*uchi ni*] usually shows the speaker's concern about what might happen. However, it may also indicate that something was done within a shorter time span than expected. Some examples of this meaning:

地震の余韻がさめやらぬうちに今度は大雨で作物に大きな被害がでた。

*Jishin no yoin ga sameyaranu uchi ni kondo wa ōame de sakumotsu ni ōkina higai ga deta.*

While we were still feeling the aftermath of the earthquake, there was a heavy downpour that caused tremendous damage to the crops.

あの人は，離婚して一年もたたぬうちに再婚してしまった。

*Ano hito wa, rikon shite ichinen mo tatanu uchi ni saikon shite shimatta.*

She remarried less than a year after getting divorced.

# ■ Sentence A のは [no wa] Sentence B ことです [koto desu]

As mentioned in the first chapter, one of the most important things when reading or writing in Japanese is to determine whether each sentence is the "A is B" type (AはBです) or the "A does B" type (AはBをします). Ignoring this principle can lead to incorrect sentences like the following:

私が休みにしたいのは、海に行きます。

*Watashi ga yasumi ni shitai no wa, umi ni ikimasu.*

わたしの仕事は手紙を配達します。

*Watashi no shigoto wa tegami o haitatsu shimasu.*

Each of these examples begins like the "A is B" type but ends like the "A does B" type. The following are correct:

私が休みにしたいのは、海に行くことです.

*Watashi ga yasumi ni shitai no wa, umi ni iku koto desu.*
What I want to do during vacation is to go to the beach.

わたしの仕事は手紙を配達することです.

*Watashi no shigoto wa tegami o haitatsu suru koto desu.*
My job is delivering the mail.

---

• のは [*no wa*] and からだ [*kara da*]

When a sentence ends with からだ, that sentence indicates the reason or cause for something that came before. Here, the の [*no*] of のは [*no wa*] is pronominal and replaces words such as 理由 [*riyū*] (reason), 原因 [*genin*] (cause), or 訳 [*wake*] (reason).

In (a), the の [*no*] is replacing 理由 [*riyū*] or 訳 [*wake*]:

---

(a) 昨日コンサートに行けなかった<u>の</u>は、仕事で忙し
かったからです。

*Kinō konsāto ni ikenakatta <u>no</u> wa, shigoto de iso-*
*gashikatta kara desu.*

I could not go to the concert yesterday because I
was busy with work.

In (b), the replaced word is 原因 [*genin*]:

(b) 熱が出た<u>の</u>は雨にぬれて風邪をひいたからでしょう。

*Netsu ga deta <u>no</u> wa ame ni nurete kaze o hiita*
*kara deshō.*

The reason I developed a fever was probably because I caught a cold after getting rained on.

If the first half of the sentence is replaced by それは
[*sore wa*] or これは [*kore wa*] or omitted entirely, the
sentence is giving a reason or cause for a previously
stated fact. Then the sentence may be translated as "It
is because…"

# ■ たしかに／たしか [tashika ni / tashika]

たしかに [*tashika ni*] is an adverb meaning "surely," but it is
also used to introduce negative statements (see page 84):

彼はたしかにいい人だけど、やっぱり好きになれない。

*Kare wa tashika ni ii hito da kedo, yappari suki ni narenai.*

I admit he is a nice person, but I just can't get myself to
like him.

たしか [*tashika*] indicates that the speaker's statement is
based on an uncertain memory:

ジューン： パーティー、いつだったかしら？
好子： たしか二十三日だったと思うけど……。

*Jūn:* *Pātī, itsu datta kashira?*
*Yoshiko:* *Tashika nijūsan-nichi datta to omou kedo ...*

June: When was the party supposed to be?
Yoshiko: I'm pretty sure it was the twenty-third.

---

- -た [-*ta*] for Future Tense

In the last example above, both speakers use the -た
[-*ta*] form even though they are talking about a future
event. This is common in statements that are based on
memory. Here is an example in which the -た [-*ta*]
form refers to the present:

A: お子さんは三人でしたね。
B: ええ、三人です。

*A: O-ko san wa san-nin deshita ne.*
*B: Ee, san-nin desu.*

A: You have three children, right (if I remember correctly)?
B: Yes, I have three children.

---

## ■ はじめ [hajime]

There are several easily confused phrases that contain はじめ
[*hajime*]. Here are their meanings, followed by some examples:

| | |
|---|---|
| はじめは [*hajime wa*] | at first, in the beginning |
| はじめに [*hajime ni*] | to begin with, first of all |
| はじめて [*hajimete*] | for the first time |
| はじめから [*hajime kara*] | from the beginning |

はじめはラッシュアワーの電車に乗るのがいやだった
けれど、やっと慣れました。

*Hajime wa* rasshu-awā no densha ni noru no ga iya datta
*keredo, yatto naremashita.*

At first, I hated riding on the train during rush hour, but I
finally got used to it.

はじめに自己紹介をします。

*Hajime ni* jiko-shōkai o shimasu.

First of all, let me introduce myself.

去年はじめて富士山に登った。

Kyonen *hajimete* Fuji-san ni nobotta.

Last year I climbed Mt. Fuji for the first time.

駄目なことははじめから分かっていました。

*Dame na koto wa* hajime kara *wakatte imashita.*

I knew from the beginning that it wouldn't work.

## ■ SENTENCE A そこで／それで [soko de / sore de]
## SENTENCE B ━━━━━━━━━━━━━━━━━━━

When そこで [*soko de*] is used as a conjunctive, it means
"accordingly," "and so," or "now":

最近、道路わきに投げ捨てられたゴミの山が問題にな
って来た。そこで近くの住民たちが集って清掃運動
を始めることにしたというわけである。

*Saikin, dōro-waki ni nagesuterareta gomi no yama ga*
*mondai ni natte kita. Soko de chikaku no jūmin-tachi ga*
*atsumatte seisō-undō o hajimeru koto ni shita to iu wake*
*de aru.*

Recently, the piles of litter along the roads have become a
problem, so people in the neighborhood have met together and decided to start a cleaning campaign.

そこで [*soko de*] may also be used to introduce a new topic to connect to the next statement:

来年の七月に、大きな展示会を開催することに決った。そこで君たちにも協力をお願いしたいのだが……。Ⓜ

*Rainen no shichi-gatsu, ōkina tenji-kai o kaisai suru koto ni kimatta. Soko de kimi-tachi ni mo kyōryoku o o-negai shitai no da ga ...*

It's been decided to have a big exhibition in July of next year. Now, I want to ask for your cooperation.

そこで [*soko de*] may sometimes be replaced by それで [*sore de*], but not always. そこで [*soko de*] emphasizes the time sequence without reference to any cause-and-effect relationship, whereas それで [*sore de*] focuses on the reason or cause. A sentence like きのう、雨にふられしまって、びしょぬれになりました。そこで風邪をひいたのだと思います [*Kinō, ame ni furarete shimatte, bishonure ni narimashita. Soko de kaze o hīta no da to omoimasu*] is awkward, because そこで [*soko de*] is explaining why the speaker caught a cold. それで [*sore de*] should be used instead. With それで [*sore de*], the second sentence is usually a natural result of the first, while with そこで [*soko de*], there may be no cause-and-effect relationship between the two sentences, and the second is usually controlled by the speaker.

In the next example, Tamura uses それで [*sore de*] to prompt Hanako to describe the result or outcome of her first statement:

花子：　きのうあの映画を見に行ったけどね、あまりこんでるのでびっくりしちゃった……。

田村：　それで？（どうしたの？）

*Hanako: Kinō ano eiga o mi ni itta kedo ne, amari konde 'ru no de bikkuri shichatta ...*

*Tamura:*   *Sore de? (Dō shita no?)*

Hanako:   I went to see that movie yesterday, but it was so crowded I couldn't believe it …

Tamura:   So, what did you do? (lit., And then?)

# ■ SENTENCE A -たばかりに [-ta bakari ni] SENTENCE B

In this pattern, sentence B is the result or outcome of sentence A. The speaker suggests that A is the sole cause for B, which is always undesirable or adversative. B usually ends with -てしまった [-te shimatta]. Some examples:

> うっかりしゃべったばかりに大変な騒ぎになってしまった。
>
> *Ukkari shabetta bakari ni taihen na sawagi ni natte shimatta.*
>
> There was a big fuss all because I made a slip of the tongue.

> 母親が乳をやらなかったばかりに動物園のおサルの子は死んでしまった。
>
> *Hahaoya ga chichi o yaranakatta bakari ni dōbutsu-en no o-saru no ko wa shinde shimatta.*
>
> The baby monkey died simply because the mother didn't breast-feed it.

# ■ SENTENCE A -てさえいなければ [-te sae inakere-ba] SENTENCE B

This pattern is used to show the speaker's regret. The first example suggests that B would have been possible if A had not actually happened. For example:

> あの事故が起きてさえいなければ間に合ったのに。
>
> *Ano jiko ga okite sae inakereba ma ni atta no ni.*
>
> If there hadn't been an accident, I would have been on time.

さえ [*sae*] may also be used with a noun, adjectival noun, or -く [*-ku*] form adjective:

僕はこの車さえあれば他には何も欲しくない。Ⓜ

*Boku wa kono kuruma sae areba hoka ni wa nani mo hoshiku nai.*

If I had this car, I wouldn't want anything else.

高くさえなければ買いたいです。

*Takaku sae nakereba kaitai desu.*

I would like to buy it if only it weren't so expensive.

# APPENDICES

Contrasting Particle Phrases

Answers to Exercises

# ■ Particle Phrases

(a) (as to a taxi driver) あそこで止めてください。
*Asoko de tomete kudasai.*
Please stop over there (because I want to get out).

(as to a house guest) あそこに止めてください。
*Asoko ni tomete kudasai.*
Please park your car over there.

(b) あそこを登っている人が見えますか。
*Asoko o nobotte iru hito ga miemasu ka.*
Can you see the person who is climbing over there?

あした、富士山に登ろうと思います。
*Ashita, Fuji-san ni noborō to omoimasu.*
I'm thinking of climbing Mt. Fuji tomorrow.

(c) 地震がおこったら建物から出るように言われた。
*Jishin ga okottara tatemono kara deru yō ni iwareta.*
I was told to go out of the building if an earthquake hits.

彼は十八才の時家を出たのだと言った。
*Kare wa jūhassai no toki ie o deta no da to itta.*
He told me that he had left home when he was 18 years old.

(d) 桜通りを (まっすぐ) 行って下さい。
*Sakura-dōri o (massugu) itte kudasai.*
Please go (straight) down Sakura Street.

桜通りまで／に行って下さい。
*Sakura dōri made/ni itte kudasai.*
Please go to (as far as) Sakura Street.

(e) 本はテーブルの上にあります。
*Hon wa tēburu no ue ni arimasu.*
The book is on the table.

その会議はどこ<u>である</u>のですか。

*Sono kaigi wa doko <u>de aru</u> no desu ka.*

Where is the conference being held?

(Where do you meet for the conference?)

(f) よほど疲れている<u>とみえて</u>、帰るとすぐ寝てしまった。

*Yohodo tsukarete iru <u>to miete</u>, kaeru to sugu nete shimatta.*

He went to bed as soon as he got home. He must be very
tired.

あそこの奥さんはご主人より年上<u>にみえる</u>。

*Asoko no oku-san wa go-shujin yori toshiue <u>ni mieru</u>.*

The wife looks older (although she is younger) than her
husband.

(g) 花子は京都<u>で生まれた</u>。　　　　　(place)

*Hanako wa Kyōto <u>de umareta</u>.*

Hanako was born in Kyoto.

花子は裕福な家<u>に生まれた</u>。　　　　(environment, fate)

*Hanako wa yūfuku na ie <u>ni umareta</u>.*

Hanako was born in a rich family.

(h) ハワイ<u>で</u>マウナケア<u>に</u>雪が<u>降った</u>。　(larger area / specific
point)

*Hawai <u>de</u> Maunakea <u>ni</u> yuki ga <u>futta</u>.*

In Hawaii, snow fell on (Mt.) Maunakea.

# ■ Answers to Exercises

## Exercise 1

Literal translation: The Buddhist statue, which the three
people, having finally received permission from the temple,
undid the cloth of and took out, was a Kannon statue that had

---

149

a mysterious smile and that was unlike the Buddhist statues they had seen before.

| Noun modifier | Modified word |
|---|---|
| やっと寺の許しを得た<br>[*yatto tera no yurushi o eta*] | 三人 [*san-nin*] |
| やっと寺の許しを得た三人が<br>　布を解いて取り出した<br>[*yatto tera no yurushi o eta san-<br>nin ga nuno o toite toridashita*] | 仏像 [*butsuzō*] |
| 今までの仏像と異なった<br>[*ima made no butsuzō to<br>kotonatta*] | 観音像 [*kannon-zō*] |
| 神秘的な笑みをうかべた<br>[*shinpi-teki na hohoemi o ukabeta*] | 観音像 [*kannon-zō*] |

## Exercise 2

1. あなたはだれですか。
   （わたしは）＿＿＿＿＿＿です。
   *Anata wa dare desu ka.*
   *(Watashi wa) ＿＿＿＿＿＿ desu.*

2. どれがあなたの本ですか。
   これ（がわたしの本）です。
   *Dore ga anata no hon desu ka.*
   *Kore (ga watashi no hon) desu.*

3. どなたが＿＿＿＿＿＿さんですか。
   わたし（が＿＿＿＿＿＿）です。
   *Donata ga ＿＿＿＿＿＿-san desu ka.*
   *Watashi (ga ＿＿＿＿＿＿) desu.*

4. その本はどうですか。
   （この本は）面白いです。
   *Sono hon wa dō desu ka?*

*(Kono hon wa) omoshiroi desu.*

## Exercise 3

1. At the latest, please come by 3:00.
2. I did buy a pen, but I didn't buy a mechanical pencil.
3. Even if I am busy, I will see him if no one else.
4. It *is* raining, but not so much that you need an umbrella.
5. I *have* met her before, but I don't know her name.

## Exercise 4

(a) あなたの家のとなりに何がありますか。
   *Anata no uchi no tonari ni nani ga arimasu ka.*

(b) あなたの家のとなりは何ですか。
   *Anata no uchi no tonari wa nan desu ka.*

(c) 教会はどこですか。
   *Kyōkai wa doko desu ka.*

(d) それはどの教会ですか。
   *Sore wa dono kyōkai desu ka.*

## Exercise 5

1. Routine
2. Progressive
3. Resultative
4. Routine
5. Progressive

## Exercise 6

1. のに [*no ni*]
2. のに [*no ni*]
3. けど [*kedo*]
4. なのに [*na no ni*]
5. けど [*kedo*]
6. だけど [*da kedo*]
7. のに [*no ni*]
8. のに [*no ni*]
9. けど [*kedo*]
10. けど [*kedo*]

**Exercise 7**

1. のに [*no ni*]
2. のに [*no ni*]
3. ために [*tame ni*]
4. ために [*tame ni*]
5. のに [*no ni*]
6. ために [*tame ni*]
7. のに [*no ni*]
8. のに [*no ni*]
9. のに [*no ni*]
10. ために [*tame ni*]
11. ために [*tame ni*]
12. のに [*no ni*]

**Exercise 8**

1. Whenever the rain clears up, a rainbow appears over this valley.
2. That supervisor is nice, but he's a terror when he gets angry.
3. When the television is too loud, the neighbors complain.
4. You should go, too. It is a very interesting movie (so I recommend it).
5. She looks much older (than her actual age) in pictures.

**Exercise 9**

1. 行くと [*iku to*]
2. かかってきたら [*kakatte kitara*]
3. おきたら or おきれば [*okitara* or *okireba*]
4. 来るなら [*kuru nara*]
5. もっていたら [*motte itara*]
6. あるなら／あったら [*aru nara/attara*]
7. できれば／できるなら [*dekireba/dekiru nara*]
8. みえないなら／みえなければ／みえなかったら
   [*mienai nara/mienakereba/mienakattara*]
9. おいしくなければ／おいしくなかったら
   [*oishiku nakereba/oishiku nakattara*]
10. うすかったら [*usukattara*]

日本語の基礎ルール
BASIC CONNECTIONS

1997年 1 月　第 1 刷発行
2000年 4 月　第 3 刷発行

著　者　　庄司香久子

発行者　　野間佐和子

発行所　　講談社インターナショナル株式会社

　　　　　〒112-8652 東京都文京区音羽 1-17-14
　　　　　電話：03-3944-6493

印刷所　　株式会社　平河工業社

製本所　　株式会社　堅省堂

© 庄司香久子 1997
Printed in Japan
ISBN4-7700-1968-8

# POWER JAPANESE SERIES

**An ongoing series of compact, easy-to-use guides to essential language skills**

## ALL ABOUT KATAKANA
カタカナ練習ノート
*Anne Matsumoto Stewart*

Learn to read and write katakana in a quick, effective way by combining them into words.

Paperback, 144 pages; ISBN 4-7700-1696-4

## ALL ABOUT PARTICLES
助詞で変わるあなたの日本語
*Naoko Chino*

The most common and less common particles brought together and broken down into some 200 usages, with abundant sample sentences.

Paperback, 128 pages; ISBN 4-7700-1501-1

## ANIMAL IDIOMS
動物の慣用句集
*Jeff Garrison and Masahiko Goshi*

A memorable explanation of idioms—all dealing with animals. Organized by zoological category with background notes and sample sentences.

Paperback, 160 pages; ISBN 4-7700-1668-9

## BASIC CONNECTIONS
**Making Your Japanese Flow**
日本語の基礎ルール
*Kakuko Shoji*

The connective expressions that facilitate the flow of ideas—how words and phrases dovetail, how clauses pair up with other clauses, and how sentences come together to create harmonious paragraphs.

Paperback, 154 pages; ISBN 4-7700-1968-8

## BEYOND POLITE JAPANESE
**A Dictionary of Japanese Slang and Colloquialisms**
役にたつ話ことば辞典
*Akihiko Yonekawa*

Expressions that all Japanese, but few foreigners, know and use every day. Sample sentences for every entry.

Paperback, 176 pages; ISBN 4-7700-1539-9

## "BODY" LANGUAGE
日本語の中の "ボディ" ランゲージ
*Jeffrey G. Garrison*

Common idioms that refer to the body through colorful colloquial expressions.

Paperback, 128 pages; ISBN 4-7700-1502-X

## COMMON JAPANESE BUSINESS PHRASES
日本語ビジネス・フレーズ集
*Compiled by Sanseido*
*Translated and Adapted by John Brennan*

A complete inventory of highly practical and socially appropriate expressions used every day in the Japanese working culture.

Paperback, 144 pages; ISBN 4-7700-2299-9

## COMMON JAPANESE PHRASES
決まり文句の辞典
*Compiled by Sanseido*
*Translated and Adapted by John Brennan*

The appropriate words—fixed expressions and phrases for every social situation explained in short essay format, complete with tips on culture and alternatives.

Paperback, 144 pages; ISBN 4-7700-2072-4

## COMMUNICATING WITH KI
**The "Spirit" in Japanese Idioms**
「気」の慣用句集
*Jeff Garrison and Kayoko Kimiya*

Over 200 idioms, all using the word *ki*, and all essential for communicating in Japanese.

Paperback, 144 pages; ISBN 4-7700-1833-9

## CORE WORDS AND PHRASES
**Things You Can't Find in a Dictionary**
辞書では解らない慣用表現
*Kakuko Shoji*

Some Japanese words and phrases, even though they lie at the core of the language, forever elude the student's grasp. This book brings these recalcitrants to bay.

Paperback, 144 pages; ISBN 4-7700-2388-X

## FLIP, SLITHER, & BANG
**Japanese Sound and Action Words**
日本語の擬音語・擬態語
*Hiroko Fukuda*
*Translated by Tom Gally*

The most common examples of onomatopoeia through sample sentences and situations—an excellent introduction to animated language.

Paperback, 128 pages; ISBN 4-7700-1684-0

# KODANSHA INTERNATIONAL DICTIONARIES

Easy-to-use dictionaries designed for non-native learners of Japanese.

## KODANSHA'S BASIC ENGLISH-JAPANESE DICTIONARY

日常日本語バイリンガル辞典

An annotated dictionary useful for both students and teachers.

• Over 4,500 entries and 18,000 vocabulary item
• Examples and information on stylistic differences
• Appendixes for technical terms, syntax and grammar

Vinyl flexibinding, 1520 pages, ISBN 4-7700-2628-5

## KODANSHA'S FURIGANA JAPANESE DICTIONARY
## JAPANESE-ENGLISH / ENGLISH-JAPANESE ふりがな和英・英和辞典

Both of Kodansha's popular furigana dictionaries in one portable, affordable volume.
A truly comprehensive and practical dictionary for English-speaking learners, and an
invaluable guide to using the Japanese language.

• Basic vocabulary of 30,000 entries   • Hundreds of special words, names, and phrases
• Clear explanations of semantic and usage differences
• Special information on grammar and usage

Hardcover, 1318 pages, ISBN 4-7700-2480-0

## KODANSHA'S FURIGANA JAPANESE-ENGLISH DICTIONARY

ふりがな和英辞典

The essential dictionary for all students of Japanese.
• Furigana readings added to all *kanji*   • Comprehensive 16,000-word basic vocabulary

Vinyl flexibinding, 592 pages, ISBN 4-7700-1983-1

## KODANSHA'S FURIGANA ENGLISH-JAPANESE DICTIONARY

ふりがな英和辞典

The companion to the essential dictionary for all students of Japanese.
• Furigana readings added to all *kanji*   • Comprehensive 14,000-word basic vocabulary

Vinyl flexibinding, 728 pages, ISBN 4-7700-2055-4

## KODANSHA'S ROMANIZED JAPANESE-ENGLISH DICTIONARY

ローマ字和英辞典

A portable reference written for beginning and intermediate students.
• 16,000-word vocabulary   • No knowledge of *kanji* necessary

Vinyl flexibinding, 688 pages, ISBN 4-7700-1603-4

## KODANSHA'S POCKET ROMANIZED JAPANESE-ENGLISH
## DICTIONARY ポケット版 ローマ字和英辞典

Compact and convenient, an ideal pocket reference for beginning and intermediate
students, travelers, and business people.

• 10,000-word vocabulary   • Numerous example sentences

Paperback, 480 pages, ISBN 4-7700-1800-2

## EFFECTIVE JAPANESE USAGE GUIDE
日本語学習使い分け辞典

A concise, bilingual dictionary which clarifies the usage of frequently confused words and phrases.

• Explanations of 708 synonymous terms    • Numerous example sentences

**Paperback, 768 pages, ISBN 4-7700-1919-X**

## THE MODERN ENGLISH-NIHONGO DICTIONARY
日本語学習英日辞典

The first truly bilingual dictionary designed exclusively for non-native learners of Japanese

• Over 6,000 headwords
• Both standard Japanese with *furigana* and romanized orthography
• Sample sentences provided for most entries
• Numerous explanatory notes and *kanji* guides

**Vinyl flexibinding, 1200 pages, ISBN 4-7700-2148-8**

## THE KODANSHA KANJI LEARNER'S DICTIONARY
漢英学習字典

The perfect kanji tool for beginners to advanced learners.

• Revolutionary SKIP lookup method    • Five lookup methods and three indexes
• 2,230 entries & 41,000 meanings for 31,000 words

**Vinyl flexibinding, 1060 pages (2-color), ISBN 4-7700-2335-9**

## KODANSHA'S COMPACT KANJI GUIDE
常用漢英熟語辞典

A functional character dictionary that is both compact and comprehensive.

• 1,945 essential *jōyō kanji*    • 20,000 common compounds
• Three indexes for finding *kanji*

**Vinyl flexibinding, 928 pages, ISBN 4-7700-1553-4**

## KODANSHA'S POCKET KANJI GUIDE
ポケット版　教育漢英熟語辞典

A handy, pocket-sized character dictionary.

• 1,006 *shin-kyōiku kanji*    • 10,000 common compounds
• Stroke order for individual characters

**Paperback, 576 pages, ISBN 4-7700-1801-0**

## A DICTIONARY OF JAPANESE PARTICLES
てにをは辞典

Treats over 100 particles in alphabetical order, providing sample sentences for each meaning.

• Meets students' needs from beginning to advanced levels
• Treats principal particle meanings as well as variants

**Paperback, 368 pages, ISBN 4-7700-2352-9**

**The best-selling language course is now even better!**

# JAPANESE FOR BUSY PEOPLE   Revised Edition

改訂版　コミュニケーションのための日本語　全3巻

*Association for Japanese-Language Teaching (AJALT)*

The leading textbook for conversational Japanese has been improved to make it easier than ever to teach and learn Japanese.

- Transition to advancing levels is more gradual.
- Kana version available for those who prefer Japanese script. Audio supplements compatible with both versions.
- English-Japanese glossary added to each volume.
- Short *kanji* lessons introduced in Volume II.
- Clearer explanations of grammar.
- Shorter, easy-to-memorize dialogues.

## Volume I

Teaches the basics for communication and provides a foundation for further study.

- Additional appendices for grammar usage.

| | | |
|---|---|---|
| Text | paperback, 232 pages | ISBN 4-7700-1882-7 |
| Text / Kana Version | paperback, 256 pages | ISBN 4-7700-1987-4 |
| Tapes | three cassette tapes (total 120 min.) | ISBN 4-7700-1883-5 |
| Compact Discs | two CD's (total 120 min.) | ISBN 4-7700-1909-2 |
| The Workbook | paperback, 184 pages | ISBN 4-7700-1907-6 |
| The Workbook Tapes | two cassette tapes (total 100 min.) | ISBN 4-7700-1769-3 |
| Japanese Teacher's Manual | paperback, 160 pages | ISBN 4-7700-1906-8 |
| English Teacher's Manual | paperback, 244 pages | ISBN 4-7700-1888-6 |

## Volume II

Provides the basic language skills necessary to function in a professional environment.

| | | |
|---|---|---|
| Text | paperback, 288 pages | ISBN 4-7700-1884-3 |
| Text / Kana Version | paperback, 296 pages | ISBN 4-7700-2051-1 |
| Tapes | three cassette tapes (total 200 min.) | ISBN 4-7700-1885-1 |
| Compact Discs | three CD's (total 200 min.) | ISBN 4-7700-2136-4 |
| The Workbook | paperback, 260 pages | ISBN 4-7700-2037-6 |
| The Workbook Tapes | three cassette tapes (total 130 min.) | ISBN 4-7700-2111-9 |
| Japanese Teacher's Manual | paperback, 168 pages | ISBN 4-7700-2036-8 |

## Volume III

Expands vocabulary and structure to bring the student to the intermediate level.

| | | |
|---|---|---|
| Text | paperback, 248 pages | ISBN 4-7700-1886-X |
| Text / Kana Version | paperback, 296 pages | ISBN 4-7700-2052-X |
| Tapes | three cassette tapes (total 200 min.) | ISBN 4-7700-1887-8 |
| Compact Discs | three CD's (total 200 min.) | ISBN 4-7700-2137-2 |
| The Workbook | paperback, 288 pages | ISBN 4-7700-2331-6 |
| The Workbook Cassette Tapes | two cassette tapes (total 100 min.) | ISBN 4-7700-2358-8 |
| Japanese Teacher's Manual | paperback, 200 pages | ISBN 4-7700-2306-5 |

## Kana Workbook

Straightforward text for quick mastery of hiragana and katakana utilizing parallel learning of reading, writing, listening and pronunciation.

- Grids for writing practice.
- Reading and writing exercises.
- Optional audio tape aids in pronunciation.

| | | |
|---|---|---|
| Text | paperback, 80 pages | ISBN 4-7700-2096-1 |
| Tape | one cassette tape (40 min.) | ISBN 4-7700-2097-X |

# JAPANESE FOR PROFESSIONALS

ビジネスマンのための実戦日本語

*Association for Japanese-Language Teaching (AJALT)*

A serious and detailed manual of the language of trade, commerce, and government. Fourteen lessons introduce common business situations with key sentences and a dialogue to illustrate proper usage.

Paperback, 256 pages  ISBN 4-7700-2038-4

# READING JAPANESE FINANCIAL NEWSPAPERS
## Revised and Updated Edition

改訂第二版 新聞の経済面を読む

*Association for Japanese-Language Teaching (AJALT)*

An innovative and comprehensive textbook for business people who need direct access to the financial pages of Japanese newspapers.

Paperback, 392 pages  ISBN 4-7700-2472-X

A new and exciting video course based on the best-selling textbook series

# JAPANESE FOR BUSY PEOPLE: THE VIDEO

改訂版 コミュニケーションのための日本語 / ビデオ

*Educational Advisor: Association for Japanese-Language Teaching (AJALT)*

Based on the best-selling *Japanese For Busy People* series, *Japanese For Busy People: The Video* has been specially created for beginner students of Japanese. The video provides a wealth of vivid images about life in Japan, and the opportunity to study basic sentence patterns and expressions in real-life situations. A stand-alone video course, it can be used independently—both for self-study and in the classroom, in tandem with the textbook, or as part of any basic course. Filmed entirely on location in Japan.

- 58-part drama series in three volumes—authentic Japanese presented in real-life business and social contexts
- Educational studio talks—essential expressions explained in plain English
- Computer graphic animations—extra usage examples in the form of short, funny cartoons
- Cultural Background—unique insights into life in Japan in every episode
- 32-page booklet—useful tips for self-study and using the videos in the classroom

After watching *Japanese For Busy People: The Video*, you will be able to do all of the following and more in natural and fluent Japanese:

## Volume I  21 episodes
- Go shopping at a famous department store—and buy exactly what you want at a price you are prepared to pay
- Ride a taxi—and tell the cabby exactly how to get there
- Phone for a pizza—and get what you want to eat delivered to your door
  50 min x 2 video tapes, VHS Stereo  NTSC: ISBN 4-7700-2188-7, PAL: ISBN 4-7700-2396-0

## Volume II  18 episodes
- Report lost or stolen property—and recover your belongings
- Make an appointment at the dentist—and tell the dentist which tooth aches
- Sing at a karaoke party—and decide for yourself which songs you want to sing
  50 min x 2 video tapes, VHS Stereo  NTSC: ISBN 4-7700-2189-5, PAL: ISBN 4-7700-2397-9

## Volume III  19 episodes
- Book into a hotel—and effectively complain when you're not happy with the service
- Talk about what you've seen on TV—and make your conversations more interesting
- Direct a full-scale sales presentation—and impress important clients
  50 min x 2 video tapes, VHS Stereo  NTSC: ISBN 4-7700-2190-9, PAL: ISBN 4-7700-2398-7

## The Video Guide
- A comprehensive and practical resource for all instructors and students using *Japanese For Busy People: The Video I, II, III*.
  paperback, 192 pages  ISBN 4-7700-2491-6